Complete Beading

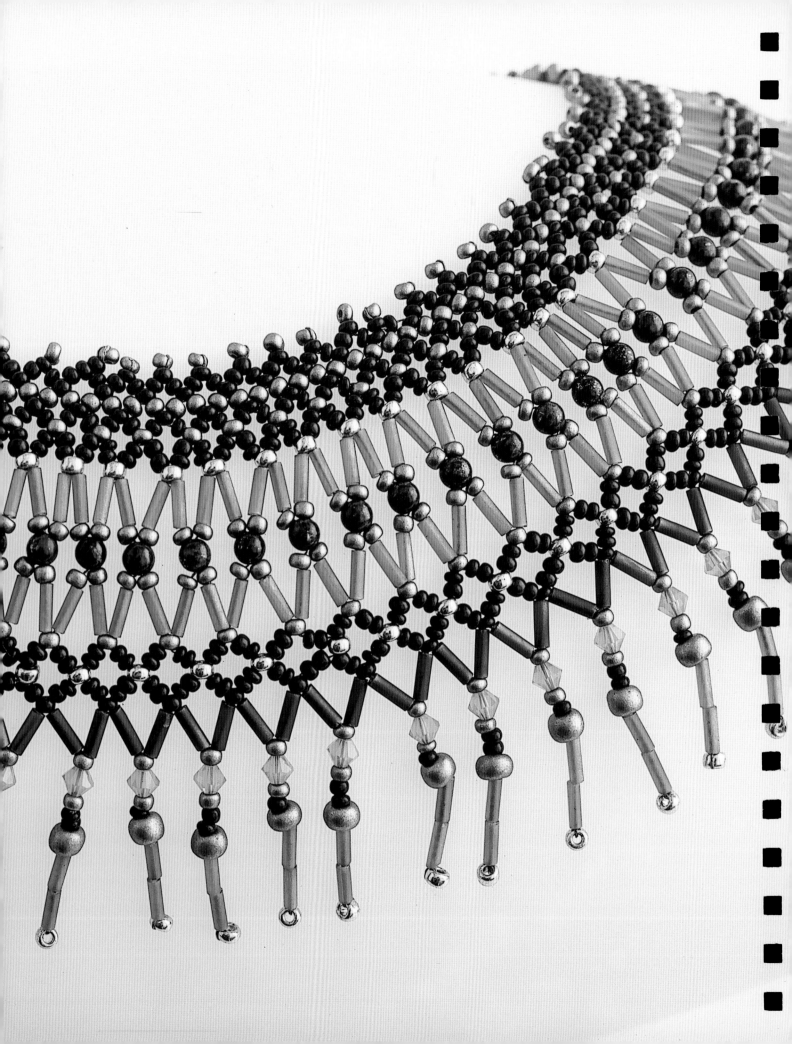

Complete
Beading

Jewelry & Accessories

Jema Hewitt

COLLINS & BROWN

This edition reprinted in 2006

Produced in 2004 by
PRC Publishing Ltd
An imprint of Anova Books Company Limited
151 Freston Road, London W10 6TH

First published in Great Britain in 2004 by
Collins & Brown
151 Freston Road, London W10 6TH

4 5 6 7 8 9 11 12 13 14

ISBN: 1-84340-239-4

Printed in Thailand

Picture credits

Cover images © Anova Image Library / Simon Clay.
All other images © Anova Image Library / Simon Clay.

Contents

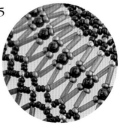

Introduction

Making a beautiful beaded creation is much like baking a tray of cupcakes. First you get simple good-quality ingredients, which often don't seem very exciting by themselves. With loving care, you mix just the right amounts of each one, in exactly the right order, using appropriate tools, such as a bowl and wooden spoon (or in the case of beading, thread and pliers). Then comes the wait, while the cupcakes bake or the beads are stitched or threaded. Finally, it's time for the most exciting part, the finishing touches; it's the icing on the cake and last embellishments that makes every piece totally unique. Of course, as with little cupcakes, it's rare that you will be satisfied with just one.

I have always been attracted like a magpie to anything that sparkles. In my youth, I loved the pots of sequins used by my mother to sew onto dance costumes, loving the way the beaded and bespangled garments came to life under the spotlight. It was a slippery slope—and I knew that one day my life would be filled to bursting with these delightful objects.

Throughout the ages, many others have loved beads, too. Lumps of honey-like Baltic amber was called "gold from the north," and could be drilled into with basic tools to form large irregular beads for prehistoric man. All types of shells were used as decoration and jewelry as early as 50,000 B.C. and cowrie shells were used in Africa as currency long before coins came into existence. In ancient Egypt, a type of rough glass called *faience* was used to create small tubular and round beads, often with different colors and patterns. These were used in conjunction with beads made from precious stones and gold to fashion incredibly complex and detailed pieces which still thrill us today.

Jewelry was also used as a ceremonial tool, marking important points in people's lives such as birth, marriage, and death. In India, large gold beads were traditionally given to a bride by her groom. The Inuit hunters even carved bone into amulets of the original animal to appease its angry spirit. A carved bead was said to have been used as a lucky amulet, to ward off evil or bring good fortune.

Right: Handmade glass beads range in size from 3–20mm.

A beaded-flower detail on a tiara by Jema Hewitt

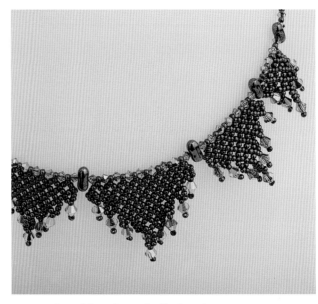

A netted necklace by Isabelle Bunting

A close-up of a necklace by Lynne Hardy

A metal necklace by Jeannette Slack

Many of these traditions continue today in some form or other. In New Orleans, long strings of beads are thrown from the famous Mardi Gras floats—this is a relatively new custom thought to have been started in 1921 by the Rex Krew.

From the ancient east of China and Japan came jade and bone, carved into exquisitely detailed beads that were sometimes used as netsuke toggles and button fastenings. Porcelain and cinnabar were made by unknown technologically advanced processes as far back as 1300 B.C. Beads made using these materials delighted other civilizations when trade routes were established. Old netsuke are particularly sought after by collectors and can fetch extremely high prices at auctions today.

As different civilizations explored the world, they discovered new lands, peoples, and materials that provided new inspiration for beading. All these cultures had exciting new products, including beads, which instantly became valuable items for trade or for gifts. I can imagine the delight with which a new bead was received, perhaps as a present from an adventurous relative.

The small size of beads made them ideal for bartering because large quantities could be carried over vast distances. The Sumerians imported lapis from Afghanistan and carnelian from the Indus valley to adorn the royal jewelry discovered at Ur. In the Elizabethan era, cargos of pearls were brought by ship to Britain by Raleigh and Drake, braving raging seas and unknown dangers, to impress their Queen. At the same time, the European explorers who first landed in the Americas took glass beads with them from their home ports as trading goods.

Glass-bead making was a trade of great mystery in Renaissance Europe. In Venice, all the glass makers were closeted away on an island and sworn to keep the guild secrets about the techniques used in creating their wonderful glass pieces and special colors. This led to a monopoly of certain techniques and very high prices, which must have enticed the ladies of Venice even more. There is quite a tradition of beaded flowers in Venice, too.

Paintings and sculptures give us a wonderful insight into the beads and jewelry worn by important figures in history. The Byzantine Empress Theodora is shown in a mosaic wearing a coronet from which strings of pearls hang on either side, framing her face. Anne Boleyn is painted toying with an unusual necklace with a dangling pendant shaped like a B. These obviously tell us very little about what ordinary people of the day may have worn as adornments, but I doubt human nature has changed very much. Cheaper versions of precious stones and metal pieces were probably worn, just as they are today.

One of the loveliest things about beads is their longevity. If made from a high-quality substance, such as semiprecious stone or crystal, they will look as good hundreds of years from now as they do today. I love to rework necklaces worn by my mother and grandmother into new designs more suitable for me. It allows me to retain the memories of the beads but create something I will actually wear. Jewelry is no good in a box—it is there to be adapted and worn.

Bead Types

There are so many types and variations of beads that only the ones used within the projects of this book are described here. Part of the pleasure in creating with beads is experimentation, so don't be afraid to try substituting one size or type of bead for another—the results may pleasantly surprise you.

Seed beads are the tiny rounded beads used for the majority of bead-weaving and embroidery projects. They are formed when a long thin tube of glass is chopped into many tiny segments and then slightly melted again to soften their edges to create a rounded rather than tubular shape. Nowadays, they are mainly made in Czechoslovakia and India.

Seeds come in a bewildering variety of sizes, colors, and finishes, and, confusingly, the higher their size number the smaller the bead! This is because the size number refers to how many beads can fit along an inch. The primary color of the bead is the color of the glass from which the cane was made; different mineral additions, such as gold and copper, change the

colors of the glass, creating rich hues. The finish of a bead refers to the final coating, which can make it iridescent, metallic, matte, pearlized, or silver-lined. The best-quality seeds are uniform in size and shape, and these are the ones you will need for most weaving and looming projects.

Miyuke delicas are a more tubular version of the seed bead; they come from Japan and are almost perfectly identical in shape and size. They knit together to form practically seamless pieces of beaded cloth when used in peyote, brick, or looming. They are also very fine and light, so although 5g may not sound like a lot, you will get an awful lot of beads in a small packet. The variety of colors and finishes for these beads is extensive.

Bugle beads are long thin tubes also cut from canes of glass; they have many of the same finishes as seed beads and, additionally, can be twisted to form little spiraled tubes. Many bugles have very sharp edges that can cut through thread, so look carefully to check the suitability of each type for your project; Japanese bugles tend to have better rounded edges. Another good tip is to put a seed bead at the top and bottom of each bugle to protect

Right: Pressed-glass flower-shaped beads can come in sizes of 6–16mm.

the thread from fraying when used in fringes or bead-weaving projects.

Many beads referred to in stores as "crystals" are, in fact, pressed glass. True crystal beads have a very high lead content in the glass from which they've been made, which increases their sparkle when cut. This adds to their price, but the obvious difference in quality makes them worth using whenever possible. The best-quality crystal beads come from Austria and are available in many sizes and faceted shapes; most popular is the bicone, which is used in many projects in the book.

Pressed-glass and fire-polished beads are created by pouring molten glass into moulds. They do not have quite the same sparkle as crystal, but they are more readily available and much cheaper, with some lovely delicate iridescent colors in the ranges. They are often a nice oval shape and come in several different sizes.

Italian glass beads are often created by millefiore canes. Millefiore means a thousand flowers, and that is just what these intricately patterned beads remind me of. To make them, tiny chunks are cut from a cane, which has a motif all the way through like a stick of rock, creating fascinating beads with lots of tiny pictures in them. Other Venetian beads have sparkling gold centers and a pretty raised-flower swirl. Venice was the center for glass innovation in the Renaissance, and many skilled workers still create within the city, handforming each bead over a torch lamp.

Lamp working is the process by which a cane of glass is melted over a hot-flamed torch and rolled around a thin metal rod to create a bead. The bead can then be further worked with the addition of

Above: Bali silver cones come in a variety of sizes from 6–20mm.

other pieces of glass from fine rods called "stringers," pieces of millefiore, gold, and silver leaf. It can even be shaped into a whimsical figure or object. These beads often serve as a focal point for a necklace. The price depends on the complexity of the design and prestige of the artist. But when you consider the skill involved in its creation, the price paid for an expensive bead could be a bargain for what is in fact a miniature work of art.

If you look closely at an unusual bead, thinking it is stone or lamp-worked glass, you may be surprised to find it is actually polymer clay. This fabulous substance can be used to mimic just about any technique of glass or finish of real stones without any special equipment. It starts out the same consistency as plastic modeling paste, and it remains pliable until baked in a regular oven. It is great fun to make your own beads with it, and excellent results can be had right from the beginning. There are several brands, each of which has its own advantages. Watch out for artists who work with polymer clay, too. They are making exquisite beads from this material that may become very collectible.

Metal beads can be either pure metals or plated. Pure silver and gold beads are often sold by weight, with the price of silver per ounce changing according to market forces. Bali has long been a source of intricate silver beads, but be careful of the quality of the beads you buy. Silver comes in different degrees of purity—sterling silver has a high amount of silver particles within its makeup and will therefore be more expensive than a bead made from low-grade ore. Different countries also have different regulations as to what percentage of silver is acceptable before something may be labeled as "silver."

A wonderful product called silver clay has now made it possible to make your own silver beads, which you can mold by hand and fire using a blow torch. The silver particles meld together with the heat, leaving the clay part to be brushed off when the bead is cool.

Cloisonné beads have a metal base with wire soldered in patterns upon the bead; the different

Above: Venetian millefiore beads, approximately 15mm in size.

areas are then filled with colored enamel. This technique was applied in ancient Egypt using gold with glass melted into the spaces, but Chinese designs predominate today.

Many natural objects have been used as beads throughout history. Some of the first beads were pebbles with a hole that were found in prehistoric graves, so it is not surprising that bones, shells, and natural seeds all remain popular as components in jewelry. Found objects can always be drilled to add a hole—however many of these natural things are brittle, as I have discovered to my cost halfway through a project. So be aware of potential fracture points before drilling and threading. Bones, nuts, and wood can all be carved to create further shapes. Wooden beads may seem the province of only ethnic-inspired projects, but these beads can also be dyed and painted to create wonderful bases for embellishment by other beads or oven-baked clay.

Pearls are among the most precious found objects. The product of an irritation in the shell of the humble oyster, most pearls are

now created by artificially inserting an irritant into shellfish farmed in vast beds in warm parts of the ocean. These irritants can be shaped so the object will be covered by the shiny nacre. Pearls were a popular wonder passed off as a natural miracle. It is also possible to remove the pearl without harming the shellfish, and this should be encouraged whenever possible in the interests of ecology.

As a natural product pearls are all unique—the most precious being perfectly round—but many shapes and shades will be found in a matching string. Fake pearls are made from glass, plastic covered, or clad with a pearl coating. Plastic and acrylic beads are a very affordable option for fun fashion projects, but pearlized coatings often do not last, and seam lines from the molding process sometimes mar the larger beads.

There are many incredible colors and patterns contained within our rocks and minerals; the color turquoise is named for a natural stone, even though it seems so far removed

Left: Lapis and malachite beads (8mm)
Above: Turquoise and jade beads (approx. 4mm)
Right: An assortment of pearls and beads

from the gray pebbles of most beaches. Beads made from semiprecious stones are just so beautiful, with their own inner glow. The choice of stones is huge; some are very expensive, some are surprisingly cheap.

Semiprecious gems are often sold in long strands on temporary thread, but many shops will sell just a few of the more expensive beads. Before you buy, check the size of the drilled hole. Sometimes it's very small, and it can be frustrating to thread your lovely gems on a large hairpin! Different shapes are often available: round, square, faceted, and even little flowers, animals, and leaves can be collected.

There are different qualities of semiprecious gems, and stones also vary enormously in color. Amethyst can come in colors from palest lavender to very dark purple; lapis lazuli can be navy or bright blue. With experience, you will be able to distinguish finer gems from lower qualities. So long as the price is fair, always choose the gem most suitable in color and shape for your project. Some stones need special care, so check with your dealer regarding how to clean and care for them.

If a gem seems to be too much of a bargain, chances are it is "reconstituted." These stones are made from dust and chips from the expensive stone, glued together with resin and reshaped. Coral and amber are often treated in this way, and many readymade jewelry pieces are reconstituted, while their labeling implies they are made of solid stone. Other gems may be dyed or heat-treated to enhance the colors. Howlite, in particular, is a popular base for a turquoise-color dye. It can be just as lovely as the real thing, but it should be labeled properly.

Left: Seed beads are available from 1½–4mm.
Right: Crystals can be 3–12mm.

Tools

They say a bad workman blames his tools, but there are some pieces of equipment without which any beading work will be much trickier. There are huge storage systems for seeds and Delicas that allow you to see each color. They are handy if you bead constantly or like to keep everything tidy, but I haven't found one necessary for my work. A small tool kit can be kept in a shoebox or an all-purpose plastic carrier, ready to be called into action when you want to bead. I'd hide it from the rest of the family, though, because the things you find most useful will inevitably disappear.

Small jewelry work pliers are essential for the neat finishing of jewelry pieces. There are several different types, and each fulfills a specific purpose. You can also buy three-in-one sets of pliers that incorporate the three main types in one tool. They are not as sturdy as separate tools, but they can be very handy if you like to travel with an in-progress project but don't want to carry everything with you.

Round-nosed pliers (bottom left) are used to create perfect circular loops. The pliers' tips are gradiated so you can make tiny loops or large ones.

Among the many uses of these loops are attaching headpins to earring findings.

Flat-nosed pliers (bottom right) have a good gripping surface for holding small pieces while you work on them. They are essential for getting a firm hold when closing jump rings, and they make neat right-angle bends in wire.

Wire cutters (bottom center) are the only things that should be used to snip any gauge of wire; even wire that seems as fine as thread will totally destroy your scissors. But don't use regular wire cutters on memory wire because it will chip the blades.

Memory-wire cutters (right) are made from

even stronger metal to cope with the added strength of this particular type of wire.

Scissors should be very sharp, because some strengthened threads can be awkward to cut neatly. A little pair of embroidery scissors are handy. Why not create a beaded string to hang around your neck so you don't lose them? Another method of trimming is by a tiny antique-style thread cutter. This is a very safe little object with a concealed round blade, but it will only handle fine threads.

Needles are another workbox essential. Flexible, large-eyed ones made from twisted wire are great for threading normal bead thread and thicker cords through medium and large beads. For seed beads, embroidery, looming, and weaving you will need a stiff, sharp needle. The eye is small, so only fine thread can be used with it. A needle threader won't go through either, so I have a handy magnifying glass, passed down through

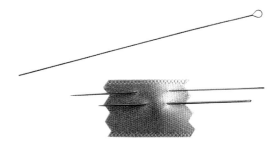

the family, which saves hours of threading frustration.

Glue is important for securing knots and attaching some findings. Cyanoacrylate dries fast and strong but also dries white, so don't get any on your beads! Specific branded bead glue takes a little longer to dry but is usually clear and strong. A dab of either of these

glues is good for securing a knot. But in a pinch, a drop of clear nail polish will also do it.

Two-part epoxy glue is incredibly strong, dries clear, and is used to attach larger components together. It takes a little while to set after mixing, so you need to arrange the pieces to stay in position until then—try a bit of masking tape to hold them together. It will hold metal, glass, crystal, and wood, as well as other materials.

Threads

Using the right thread will make or break a project, if you will excuse the phrase. There are many different types and even more different brands of each type, but you will soon find your own personal favorites and the ones most suited to your creations. Don't be afraid to try new threads, too; I have become a convert to several types after listening to a friend's recommendation.

Conditioners, which come in a little pot like a lip gloss, and traditional beeswax will strengthen threads, helping them resist tangles and remain strong. You just run the thread along the conditioner, from end to end, holding it firmly against the wax with your finger so every bit gets coated. Beeswax can make thread quite stiff, so do use it with caution.

Nylon bead threads (1) are strong and used for both straightforward stringing and looming projects. Light and flexible, they come in skeins of many colors. Fine beading thread is used in bead-weaving projects when the thread has to pass through tiny

1

seed beads or Delicas several times. It is stronger than sewing thread and easily threaded on a sharp needle.

Plastic-coated metal wire is extremely strong but can kink and bend in long lengths, so it is only suitable for straightforward stringing projects. Most types are too stiff to knot but can be crimped to secure clasps. There are many thicknesses and colors of plastic-coated wire with which to play.

2

Monofilament (5), nylon bead wire, and fishing wire are all-plastic threads. They are mainly used for intricate Japanese crystal weave projects and illusion necklaces, where tiny beads hang in swathes with no apparent thread to hold them. It is not suitable for basic threading but is often used on

3

cheaper
bracelets or
necklaces sold
to tourists. If you buy
beads abroad, thread them as soon as possible
to avoid breakages.

Natural fiber cords (2) and (3) are an obvious
choice for large natural beads and pendants.
Thick cotton, hemp, silk, and leather all give a
defined shape to a project. They can be knotted
or braided to give texture, and there are faux
versions of suede and leather, if you prefer. Cords

may also be plaited or embellished with Chinese
knots for extra texture.

Wire (4) is not really suitable for the basic threading
of beads. Wire is used for creating findings, (page
22), such as eyepins and jump rings, and for special
projects, such as tiaras. It is available in solid silver
and gold, as well as plated metals. The gauge of a
wire refers to its thickness in diameter and is usually
measured in inches. Memory wire has been treated
by heat so that it returns to its original rounded coil
even when pulled out of shape. It is available in
several different sizes for necklaces, rings, and
bracelets.

Chains are also made by joining small links of wire
together. Different styles of joining the links result in
assorted patterns such as "trace" and "rope" chains.
Most stores sell it by the inch for use in
projects or you can just add a clasp and use the
finished neck chain to hang a special pendant.

4

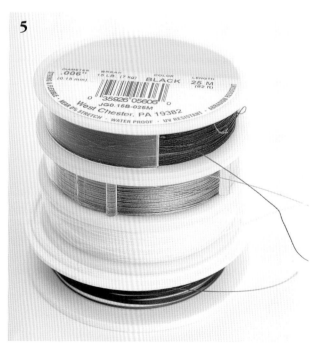

5

Findings

Findings is the general phrase used for all those handy odds and ends that finish off a piece of jewelry. Very elaborate pieces are available, as well as classic shapes. Look for old or broken necklaces with lovely clasps or spacers; you can give a vintage finding a whole new lease on life with some fresh new beads, or a gorgeous clasp may finish off a great new design with style. Findings can be found in sterling silver and pure gold, as well as plated metals and some colored steels.

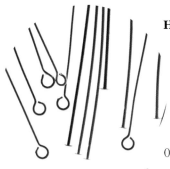

Headpins and eyepins are essential for earrings and can also make useful components in necklaces. You can make eyepins very easily with a piece of 0.6mm wire and a loop made from round-nosed pliers, but headpins are best purchased ready-made. They look like dressmaking pins with no point and can be bought in an assortment of thicknesses and lengths, as well as assorted metals; some even have decorative heads.

Necklace ends are also called **calottes** and look like tiny clamshells. They are used to conceal the knot or end of a string and connect it to the clasp. They give a more professional finish than tying beads to a clasp with a visible knot. Thong ends are slightly larger and

provide a neat finish for leather and thicker cords.

Crimp beads are tiny tubes of metal that are squashed on the end of a wire using flat pliers to hold the beads in place. They are often used inside a necklace end instead of a knot when threading plastic-coated metal wire.

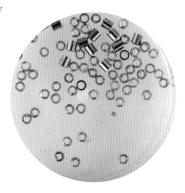

Jump rings are tiny circles of wire used to join components together. They are available in different sizes, or you can make your own by winding wire around a knitting needle and then snipping down one side of the spring with wire cutters. Luckily, the rings will already be twisted open and be ready for your use.

I must admit that I get a bit carried away when I see **unusual clasps**, as they make so much difference to the final look of a piece. Some are just so gorgeous that I've used them as the central focal point as well as the fastening.

T-bar clasps are definitely a favorite for bracelets because they are easy to fasten with one hand. For the best security, it's hard to beat a simple lobster clasp. Both multiholed clasps and pretty cones are nice ways to combine multiple strands of a necklace down to one point for fastening.

Spacer bars keep different rows of beads separate from each other around the necklace. There are huge chunky bars that make bold statements and tiny thin ones you'd hardly know were there; some have holes placed far apart for big beads, and some are quite close. Check the distance between them to make sure your beads will sit in neat rows.

Because some people are allergic to base metal and can only wear pure gold or sterling silver through their ears, and others don't have pierced ears, it is just as well there are plenty of different types of earring wire available. The basic shape is that of a fish hook that goes through the ear. The bottom ring can be twisted open and shut to add a beaded headpin. There are many variations, including types for nonpierced ears, so find the ones that you think are most comfortable.

Bead Threading

There is nothing more beautiful than a length of gorgeous beads simply threaded either as a single strand or multiple strands of cascading pieces. My philosophy is, why create complicated woven pieces when you can let the lovely beads do the work? So long as you choose good-quality beads and the right thread for them, your creation will give you pleasure for many years.

In Nepal many strands of seed beads in auspicious colors of red or yellow are offset with necklaces of silver coins strung simply together on thick cord. Big hanks of seed beads can look wonderful just as they are, and I am often tempted by the long semiprecious strands hung together on temporary thread in the store. They just look so gorgeous, in every color of the rainbow saying "buy me, buy me." So, of course, I do.

But what to do with all of these glorious beads? Well, you can thread beads in all sorts of patterns to create a unique piece of jewelry. A symmetrical design usually works its way equally from a large central focus. A random design is a personal selection of totally different beads that often vary in either in color or shape. An asymmetrical piece has a focus on one side of the design, and a repeating pattern uses a sequence of beads again and again.

A deeply grooved beading board allows you to layout your design before stringing, which saves lots of time and energy chasing beads as they roll off the table. A board also enables you to shift beads around and play with ideas before deciding on a final pattern and length.

Different lengths of necklace will either enhance a neckline or be hidden by it. Short and choker lengths look great with strapless summer dresses, open neck blouses, or V-necks sweaters. For a high-neck sweater, make sure the necklace will comfortably cover the neckband and hang where it will show. Very long necklaces are certainly eye catching but are best worn with evening wear because they can get in the way while you're working. I like to wrap my favorite long necklaces several times around my wrist for an instant daytime alternative.

The right clasp can really enhance a simple finished project. There are many different styles of clasps, but personal preference has a lot to do with your final choice. I always favor an enormous sparkly clasp, but some prefer a discreet little catch that doesn't distract the eye. On a bracelet, make sure you can fasten it with one hand— unless you have a ladies' maid of course! If your piece is long or is threaded on elastic, then you will not need a clasp at all.

Different types and weights of bead will need different threads to make a longlasting necklace; I use the term thread to cover everything from wire to cord. I always keep a large selection in my workbox, ready to whip out the second I spot some new beads.

Above: A turquoise heart bracelet

As a rough rule of thumb, always try to use the thickest thread that will go through the hole, although some of the thinner plastic-coated wire threads are extremely strong.

Elastic, though convenient, will always stretch over time. Some other threads will stretch over a long period too, leaving you with a bit of thread showing near the clasp. To avoid this, use a no-stretch thread. If it does happen you will need to

Left: A oven-baked clay pendant hung from thick cord

re-thread the whole piece. Some beads, such as a knotted strand of pearls, should be re-strung on a regular basis anyway to make sure they are always secure and that the thread is not frayed.

Different fibers will also drape differently. A stiff thread will not create a particularly soft and flowing necklace. A fine cotton strand will not support a chunky stone choker in a pleasing shape. Sometimes you will have to try again with a different type, but don't be too upset because you're always building up a valuable store of knowledge about threads and beads.

A common mistake is to leave insufficient slack in the filament when attaching the clasp. If you pull the thread too tight on a completely beaded piece, the beads will lock together, creating a stiff and unwieldy piece of jewelry. The solution is to

experiment to see just how tight to pull the thread. Try holding it in a curve while you tie on the clasp pieces or wrapping it around a tube the correct size.

Beading needles can make stringing so much easier, especially on those days when you feel as if you have two left hands. They come in a bewildering variety—the most useful in my opinion are the twisted wire type with a collapsible eye, as you can thread it up very easily through its large eye and then the eye compresses to get through the bead. These fit through most holes, although seed beads need a stiff, fine beading needle to thread easily.

Some stiffer threads won't need a needle, but if you're really having trouble, you can always put a bit of glue on the end. When the glue is dry, cut the thread at a sharp angle and you have your own built-in needle!

Basic Bead-Threading Techniques

Necklace ends

1 To close a crimp, hold it between the jaws of a pair of flat-nosed pliers and squeeze until it is flat.

OR

2 Tie a large knot, or even two or three knots, and then trim the ends.

Thread on a necklace end, and close very gently with flat-nosed pliers around the crimp or knot.

Leather ends

Place a dab of glue on the end of the cord; then close each side of the clamp one after another with flat-nosed pliers.

Headpin loop

1 Grip the round-nosed pliers about 1" from the top of the wire.

2 Twist the pliers through 90 degrees away from you, creating a right angle.

3 With your free hand, curve the top piece of wire back toward you, shaping it tightly over the top of the pliers.

4 Keep curving until it crosses the other piece of wire, and remove the round-nosed pliers.

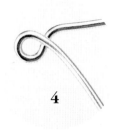

4

5 Slide the wire cutters inside the loop so that the cutting edge is flush with the inside edge of the wire circle, and snip.

5

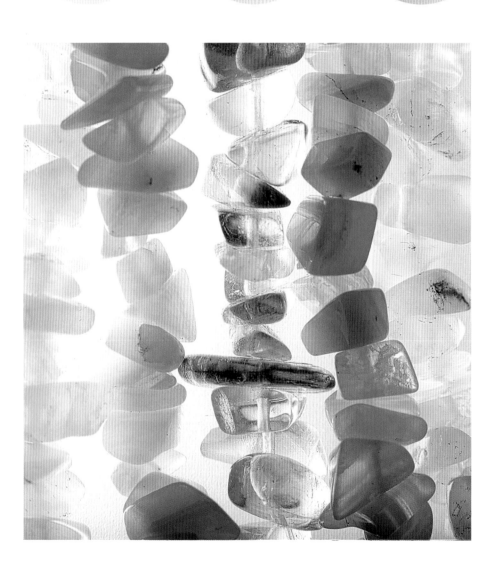

Wrapped loop

1 Grip the round-nosed pliers about 1" from the top of the wire.

2 Twist the pliers through 90 degrees away from you, creating a right angle.

3 With your free hand, curve the top piece of wire back toward you, shaping it tightly over the top of the pliers.

4 Keep curving until it crosses the other piece of wire, and remove the round-nosed pliers.

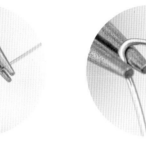
1

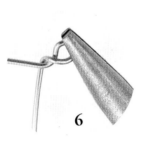
2

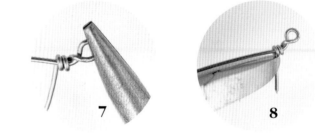
3

4

5 Grip the loop with flat-nosed pliers.

6 Start wrapping the tail around the stem wire very neatly.

7 Wrap three times, and close together.

8 Snip close to the stem.

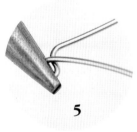
5

6

7

8

Opening and closing jump ring

1 Hold each side of the ring with pliers, and twist. Do not pull apart, or it will not return to a perfect circle.

2 To close, grip each side with pliers and twist back again.

1

2

Knots

Square or reef knot (for two ends)

1 Cross the left-hand thread over the right-hand thread, and wrap right around.

2 Cross the right-hand thread over the left-hand thread. Pull up through the hole. Tighten the knot.

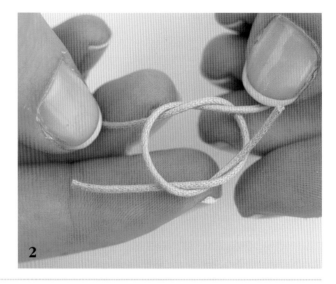

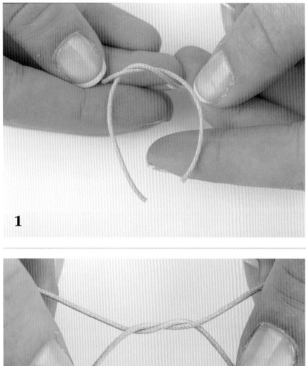

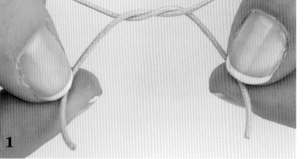

Surgeon's knot (for two ends)

1 Cross the left-hand thread over the right-hand thread, and wrap right around.

2 Now cross the right-hand thread over the left-hand thread, and pull up through the hole.

3 Wrap underneath, and pull up through the hole again.

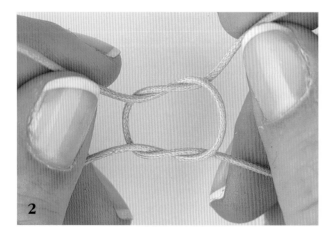

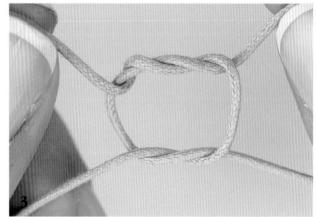

Overhand (for one end)

Make a loop with the thread; curve the thread around; and pass back through the loop. Pull tight.

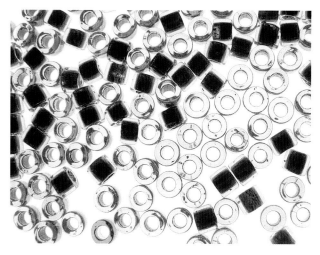

Stopper bead

1 Thread on a small bead using a needle from right to left, and pass the needle back through the bead from right to left again, creating a loop.

2 Repeat once or twice for a firmer stop; be careful not to pass the needle through the thread, just the bead.

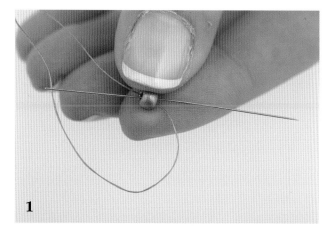

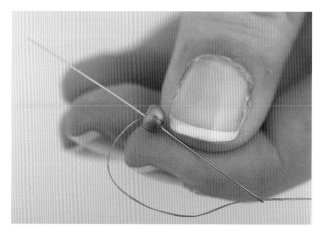

Art-Bead Pendant Necklace

This gorgeous pendant caught my eye immediately, reminding me of a butterfly wing with its iridescent sheen. While toying with different design ideas, I eventually decided I wanted to keep the setting simple so as not to detract from the pendant. I also wanted to reflect the horizontal lines patterning the glass. The faux suede provides a nice matte texture that contrasts beautifully with the extreme sheen of the glass and the lines of Delicas. The pendant itself was made from fused dichroic glass by glass artist Jan Wilcox.

Materials:

Fused-glass pendant
Faux-suede strips in lengths of 17", 20", and 22"
Plastic-coated metal wire in lengths of 18", 19", and 21"
⅛ ounce each of three colors of Delica beads
Two necklace ends
Five crimps
Two coiled-leather ends
Three 5mm jump rings
Lobster clasp

Equipment:

Flat-nosed pliers
Round-nosed pliers
Wire cutters
Glue

Instructions

1 Thread the three pieces of plastic-coated metal wire through the necklace end, and then pass them through a crimp. With the flat-nosed pliers, crush the crimp and close the necklace end as described in basic techniques. Close the top loop of the calotte with round-nosed pliers.

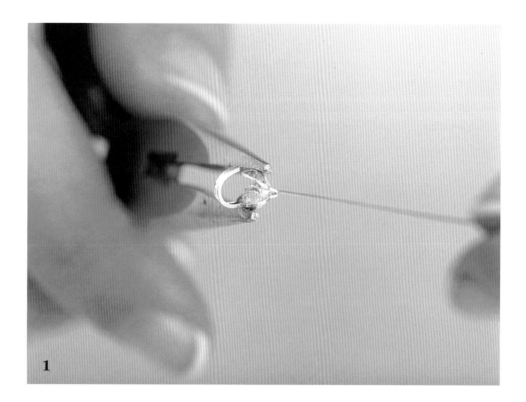

2 Thread each length of plastic-coated metal wire with a different color of Delica; keep threading them on, all the way up to 1" from the wire's end. Place and crush a crimp on the very tip of each length as you finish, so the beads don't all fall off while you are threading the others.

3 Carefully hold all three threaded ends level; keep your fingers gripping tightly above the beads; and snip off the crimp with wire cutters. Carefully thread the three wires through the other necklace end, and finish with a crimp as before. Shut the necklace end, and close its loop.

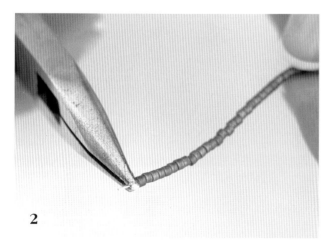

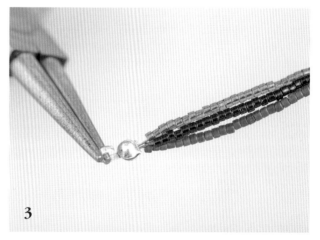

4 Place the ends of the three suede strips in the leather finding. With a pair of flat-nosed pliers, squeeze the bottom coil of the wire until it grips the suede very tightly. Thread the pendant onto the longest piece of suede, and finish all three pieces, as before, on the other side using the second leather end.

5 Open a jump ring, and thread on one of the leather ends, a calotte end, and a lobster clasp. Repeat on the other side, but include a second jump ring instead of the lobster clasp.

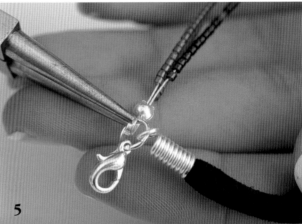

Bead Anklet

The understated elegance of this charming anklet comes from carefully choosing a palette of contrasting but pleasing small glass beads from which to thread. To make a palette of beads, take a little clear pot and start putting a selection of four or five of each bead in it. Choose two shades within your color scheme, such as lavender and plum. Although both of these might be considered purple, they are different, in fact. Stick to beads that fall within those two shades. Keep checking your blend, and take out any beads that look unpleasant. You now have a beautiful selection from which to paint your thread.

Materials:

Silver T-bar clasp
Two silver crimps
Two silver necklace ends or calottes
13" of 0.015mm plastic-coated metal wire
Approximately 27 x 4mm beads and crystals of assorted shapes
Approximately 27 x 5mm beads and crystals of assorted shapes

Equipment:

Flat-nosed pliers
Round-nosed pliers
Wire cutters

Instructions

1 First thread a crimp onto the end of the plastic-coated metal wire, and gently squeeze with the pliers to crush, as described in basic techniques. Make sure it grips firmly and will not move.

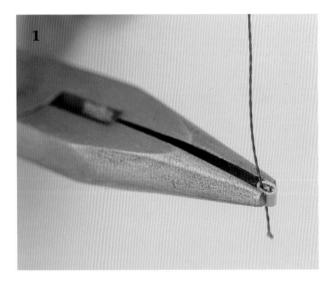

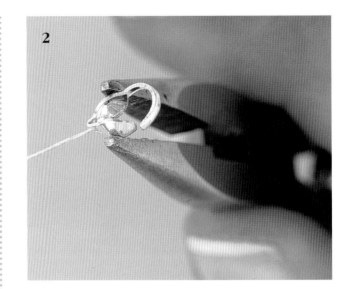

2 Thread on a calotte to cup the crimp like a pearl in an oyster shell. Very gently, close the necklace end with flat-nosed pliers.

3 Thread on all the beads in a random pattern, but try to make sure no identical colors or shapes are next to each other. Get a nice mix of the two shades, but don't feel they have to be alternate.

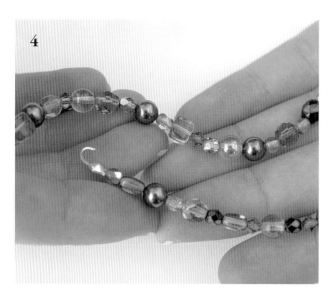

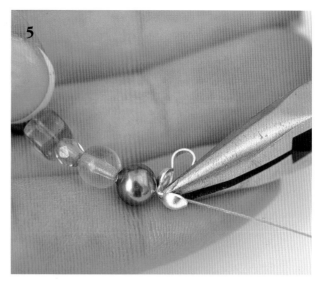

4 Check the length of the anklet, and add or sub-tract beads as necessary. Remember: there will be an extra ½" on the length from the addition of the clasp.

5 Thread on the calotte and the crimp. With the tips of your pliers, crush the crimp leaving a ¼" gap between it and the last bead to allow the anklet to hang properly. Snip off any leftover wire with a pair of wire cutters. Close the calotte gently once more.

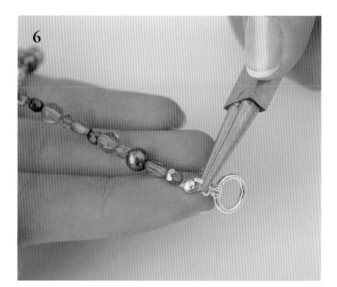

6 Attach the clasp by gently closing the necklace-end attachment with a pair of round-nosed pliers.

Name Bracelet

When a friend brought me these roses and leaves beads back from New York, I immediately thought of my mother, whose name is Dorothy Rose. I was taken back to my childhood and could almost smell the huge pink climbing roses that bloomed at the windows every June. So I designed a bracelet just for her. These bead roses climb up memory wire, a useful material that not only expands to fit most wrists but also needs no clasp to fasten it.

Materials:

Four coils of memory wire
Two headpins
Seven round rose beads
Square sterling-silver name beads
10 glass leaves
Nine 1" curved spacing beads
Approximately 30 small gold beads
Approximately 10 peridot tumble chips
Six small frosted flowers
Two large frosted flowers
Two pink hearts
Two 5mm pink crystals
Two 5mm red crystals
Six 4mm red fire-polished beads

Equipment:

Memory-wire cutters
Flat-nosed pliers
Round-nosed pliers
Wire cutters

Instructions

1 Grip the very end of one piece of memory wire with a pair of round-nosed pliers, and curve it upward. It will be very stiff, but try and make a complete tiny round loop. Put aside four tumble chips, four gold beads, two round rose beads, two small flowers, and two red fire-polished beads.

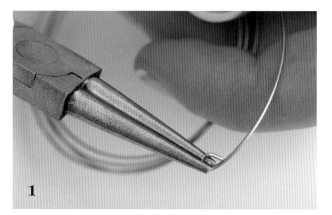

2 Now place a gold bead on each end of the curved spacing bead and a leaf on each side of the round rose bead. Push the beads down to the end of the wire. Thread a gold bead between each letter bead, and create symmetrical clusters with the frosted flowers, crystals, and tumble chips. Keep threading until you have only ½" left on the memory wire.

3 Make another loop at the end of the bracelet with a pair of round-nosed pliers, snipping off any excess memory wire before you start.

4 Take the beads you had put aside earlier, and thread them on to each of the headpins with a gold bead, fire-polished, flower, gold, peridot, round rose, and another peridot. Make a loop as described in basic techniques, but don't trim the end.

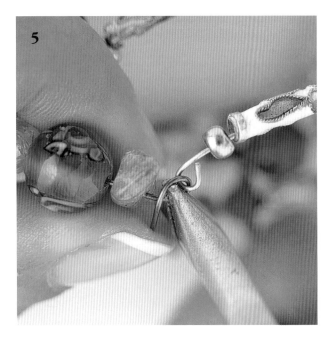

5 To finish off the dangles, hook the loop from the headpin into a memory wire end loop and make a wrap as described in basic techniques.

Pastel Seed Pearl Bracelet

Pearls always look luxurious, and these dyed seed pearls have a chic contemporary feeling, as well. They remind me of the beautiful colored puffed rice cakes I ate as a child. All sorts of colors are available, usually with a glorious iridescent sheen. I loved the way they looked in a heap together so I decided to strand loads together just for fun. Knotting between every bead is usually done with expensive stones to avoid loss if the string breaks and they all tumble off. It is also a neat and secure way to add French wire to the end of a strand. This wire, otherwise known as gimp, protects the thread from wear and gives a professional finish.

Materials:

Two 16" strands of colored rice pearls
12 x ½" silver gimp/French wire
Five 3mm crystals to match pearls
Seven 4mm crystals to match pearls
Three strand silver clasp
Strong nylon bead thread

Equipment:

Sharp needle
Scissors

Instructions

1 Cut 20" of thread, and make two knots on top of each other, about 3" from the end of the thread.

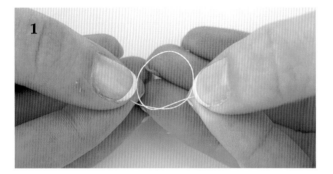

2 Thread a long sharp needle with this length. Thread on three pearls and a piece of gimp. Next, thread through one of the holes in the clasp, and pass the needle down through the first pearl.

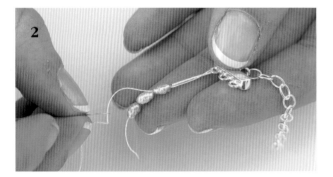

3 Make a knot around the thread between the two pearls, and pull it tight. It should be large enough so the pearl can't pass over it but small enough to look neat. Thread down through the next pearl, and make another knot.

4 Thread the needle through the final pearl; make a knot over the first knots; and thread on the rest of the pearls, interspersing them with the occasional crystal (of either size) until you have the right length for the bracelet.

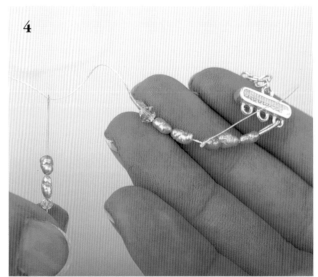

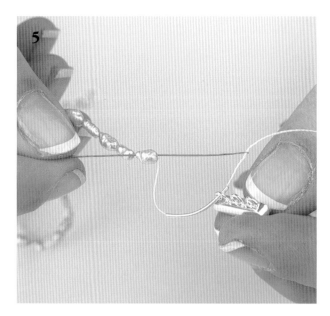

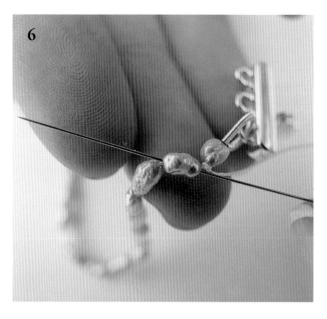

5 To finish the other side, thread on a piece of gimp and the other end of the clasp. Thread the needle back down through the last pearl.

6 Make a knot, and pass the needle down through the next pearl along; knot; thread down; and knot. Finally thread down through three or four more pearls. Trim the end of the thread.

7 Returning to the loose thread on the other side, thread it down through three or four pearls, and trim the end. Repeat the stringing six times, placing two strands of pearls through each hole of the clasp.

Cluster Earrings

*While I admit the 1950s may not have been a wonderful time for women's
liberation, I just adore the clothes and accessories. Picture the perfect little
woman, bustling around the home looking pretty in pastels. If you feel a more
sophisticated look is for you, team these earrings with a chiffon scarf wrapped
around in movie-star style and the classic Monroe sunglasses. Perforated findings are
often used in vintage jewelry to create huge clusters of beads in a neat and secure fitting.
If you'd like to make a matching set, look for them to create necklace
clasps and brooches using the same pattern.*

Materials:

24 x 4mm crystals
12 Delica beads
12 freshwater pearls
Two 20" of nylon fishing wire
Two perforated findings
Two clips on backs

Equipment:

Scissors
Flat-nosed pliers
Glue

Instructions

1 Thread a length of nylon through center hole of a perforated finding; leave a 2" tail at the back to tie off later. On the front end, thread on a crystal and a Delica. Go back through the crystal, and pass the thread through a different hole. Make sure you hold the thread securely as you work to stop the ends slipping back from the holes.

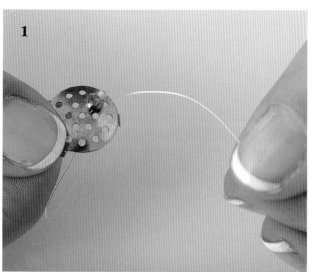

2 Bring the nylon up through the next hole; repeat the threading pattern; and take the nylon back down through center hole. Pull firmly to sit the crystal nicely against the finding.

3 Repeat this threading pattern until there is a cluster of six crystals in the center.

4 Thread on alternate pearls, crystals, and Delicas, using the edge holes of the finding. Thread this pattern all the way round the central cluster, ending by threading the wire to the back of the finding.

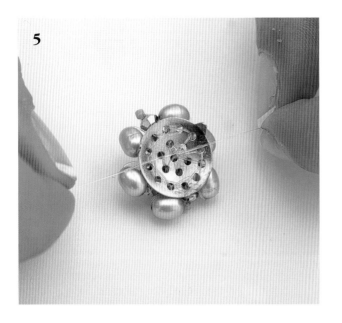

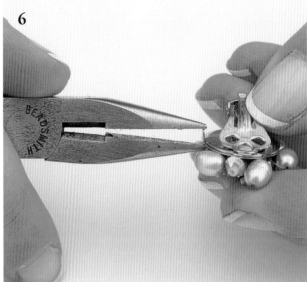

5 Tie off the nylon at the back with a square knot and put a dab of glue on the knot. Trim off any extra length.

6 Place the finding onto the earring back finding and close the little flaps gently shut with pliers to secure the pieces together. Now make a second for a matching pair.

Strand and Art-Bead Necklace

These gorgeous silver-lined glass beads have been acid-etched to give them a dreamy matte sheen. Because they are flat, they are not bulky when worn despite their large size. The colors are so subtle within the beads, I thought they'd get lost if strung with other large beads. So I used many strands of tiny seeds and Delicas to give a soft and subtle edge to the necklace. I was particularly pleased with the cylinder end beads that I tried in desperation after deciding all my cones were just too big. They do a fine job of hiding all the thread ends, while looking very attractive.

Materials:

Fine nylon thread
Thread conditioner or beeswax
Bali silver clasp
Two large cylindrical beads or cones that match
the clasp
Two 3" lengths of 0.6mm wire
Three ¾" art beads
Six 5mm crystals
⅛ ounce each of four color-coordinated seeds
and bugles

Equipment:

Needle
Scissors
Flat-nosed pliers
Round-nosed pliers
Wire cutters
Glue

Instructions

1 Cut about 25" of the thread and rub it through the conditioner to give it extra strength. Thread up the needle and place a firm stopper bead 3" from the end, as described in basic techniques.

2 Thread on 3½" of your first color of small beads, then thread on a crystal, an art bead, a crystal, and then 2½" of small beads. Repeat from the first crystal and finish with another crystal, art bead, and crystal.

3 Finally, thread on another 3½" of beads, and finish off the string with a very firm stopper bead. Trim the end of the thread to 3". Repeat the sequence from step 1 with another color of seed bead, passing the needle through the same crystals and art beads that are strung on the first thread. Don't count the number of seed beads because they will be slightly different sizes—rely on your measurements to keep the seed parts similar lengths.

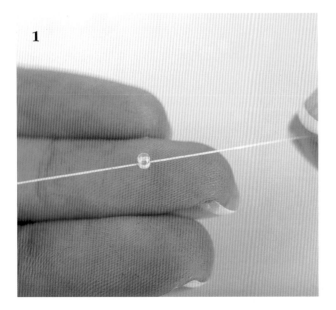

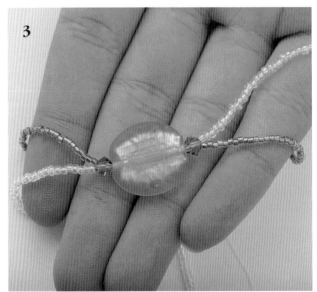

4 When all nine strands are threaded, gather one set of end threads and carefully tie them all together very close to the beads. Repeat on the other end.

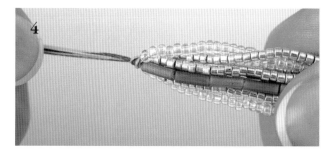

5 Create a wrapped loop with the 0.6mm wire as described in basic techniques. Pass the thread ends through the eye, and tie firmly. Place some bead glue on the knot, and when it is dry, trim the ends.

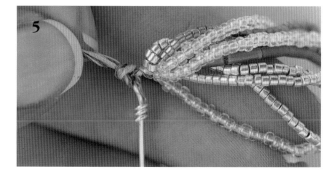

6 Thread the eyepin up through a cylindrical bead or cone, and create a nice neat loop at the top.

7 Thread one end of the clasp through the loop, and create the wrapped section. Repeat from step 5 on the other side to complete the clasp sections.

Vintage-Style Tassel Earrings

In the 1920s, when women cut their hair for the first time into the short bobbed style, long tassel earrings were much in demand. The designer Erté used long-beaded tassels extensively in his couture dress designs for the rich and famous ladies of the jazz age. The long strings of tiny beads rippled and sparkled as these sirens danced their way through the tango and foxtrot, reflecting the movement. These tassels are not incredibly long, but feel free to create a more dramatic earring tassel of 4 or even 6 inches if you dare!

Materials:

12 x 4mm crystals
Two ¾" silver cones
Two 4mm round semiprecious beads
Four bead caps
1 ounce of seed beads in three varieties
Two 2" lengths of 0.2mm silver wire
Two fish hooks
Fine nylon thread
Thread conditioner

Equipment:

Flat-nosed pliers
Round-nosed pliers
Wire cutters
Needle
Scissors

Instructions

1 With one length of the 0.2mm wire, make a neat wrapped loop as described in the section on basic techniques.

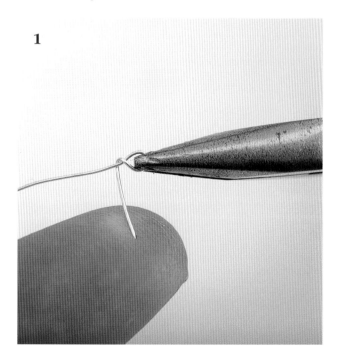

2 Now cut a 30" length of nylon thread, and pass it through the conditioner to strengthen it. Thread one end of it through the wire loop, and make a square knot to secure.

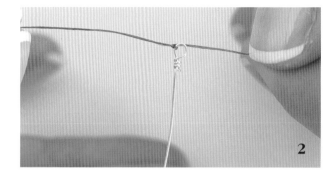

3 To make the tassel, thread on 2" of seed beads and put a crystal at the bottom. Add a seed bead, which will act as a stop bead, and thread the needle back up through the crystal and other seeds.

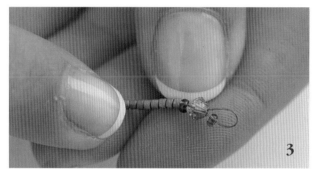

4 Take the needle through the wire loop at the top, and continue the fringe with a different type of seed bead. Make six fringe strands in this fashion, adding a sparkling crystal at a different place in the sequence each time.

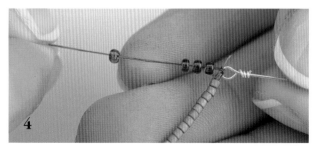

5 On the final strand, wrap the thread through the wire loop several times and tie off with a knot. Trim the end to ¼".

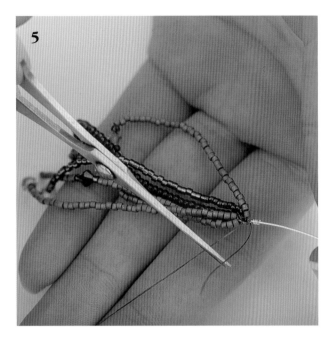

6 Onto the eyepin thread a cone, a bead cap, a round bead, and another bead cap. Make another wrapped loop at the top.

7 To attach the fish hooks, twist the loop open, just like a jump ring, then thread on the wrapped loop and twist it back to close.

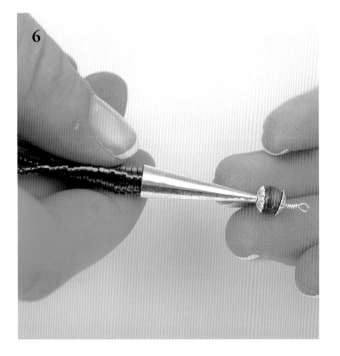

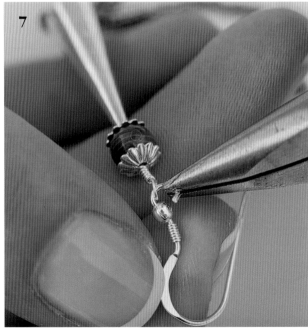

Beaded Belt

*Rabbits are considered bearers of good fortune in many cultures—when
I see them happily leaping around the fields on a spring morning I certainly
feel fortunate. Jade is also considered to be auspicious by the Chinese and
Aztec civilizations, so this belt just has to be lucky. Beaded belts are
simple to create because they are really just a longer necklace design. They are
obviously quite fragile, so be careful in your choice of extra-strong thread
for stringing. When you attach the clasp, make sure it's really secure.*

Instructions

1 Cut a 66" length of bead thread, and on one end thread on a wire beading needle. On the other end tie several knots, one on top of each other until they won't pull through a necklace end. Put a dab of glue on the knot and thread on a calotte.

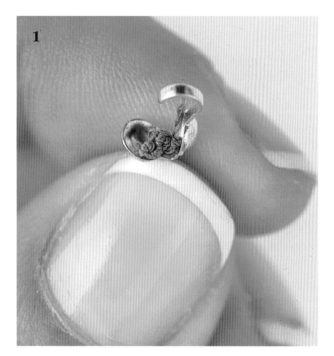

2 Thread on 1½" of seed beads then a fire-polished, crystal, FP, then another 1½" of seeds, a FP, red cloisonné, FP, seeds, FP, gold cloisonné, FP, seeds, crystal, seeds, FP, red cloisonné, FP, seeds, FP, gold cloisonné, FP, seeds, FP, heart, FP, seeds, FP, oblong cinnabar, FP, seeds, and FP.

Materials:

1" jade rabbit
Oblong cinnabar bead
Triangular cinnabar bead
Gold luck charm
Two gold hearts
Two cinnabar rose beads
Six gold cloisonné beads
Four red cloisonné beads
40 x 4mm red fire-polished beads (FP)
½ ounce size 10 red seed beads
Five 8mm crystals
Two necklace ends
Lobster clasp and jump ring
No-stretch nylon bead thread

Equipment:

Flat-nosed pliers
Round-nosed pliers
Wire cutters
Scissors
Needle
Glue

3 Thread on a gold cloisonné, fire-polished, crystal, rabbit bead, fire-polished, oblong cinnabar, fire-polished, 1" seeds, triangular cinnabar, fire-polished, ½" seeds, and the charm. Now thread the needle back up through the last fire-polished, creating a loop of seeds from which the charm hangs free.

4 Retrace the path of the original thread back up through all the beads as far as the last gold cloisonné bead. Thread on a fire-polished, and continue threading symmetrically as for the first side. When you get to the top, continue the pattern sequence, adding in the two remaining cloisonné beads. This will ensure that the rabbit tassel dangles to one side, even though the clasp is at the back.

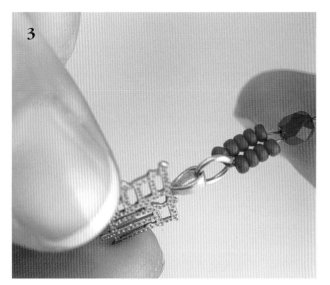

5 Thread on a necklace end, and knot as before. Close the necklace end, and add a clasp on one side and a jump ring on the other, closing the necklace end with round-nosed pliers as described in basic techniques.

Marcasite Watchband

Why have a watch that is just practical when you can have one that is both practical and beautiful? It is suggested that the jeweler Cartier invented the wristwatch, and certainly by the 1920s beaded watchbands were very popular. I have endeavored to keep the spirit of the Art Deco age alive in this glittering piece. Platinum set with diamonds was the most sought after combination for the wealthy flapper, but as I don't have the wallet of the Rockefellers, this one is mainly marcasite and shiny black onyx, with crystals, pearls, and gold-leaf beads for extra decadence.

Materials:

Watch face
A four-hole clasp
Four 5mm black onyx round beads
Two 1" flat art beads
½ ounce of size 7 seeds
16 x 4mm gold crystals
16 x 4mm silver crystals
12 x 4mm hematite crystals
Eight black rice pearls
Four lengths of 14" 0.015mm plastic-coated metal wire
Eight tubular crimps

Equipment:

Flat-nosed pliers
Round-nosed pliers
Wire cutters

Instructions

1 Take two strands of plastic-coated metal wire, and thread them both through the loop on one side of the watch face. Thread on a hematite crystal on each side, passing onto both of the threads.

2 Choose a wire from each side of the watch face and thread on a seed bead, a silver crystal, and a seed on each. Next, pass both these threads through the art bead. Thread on a seed, a silver crystal, and a seed on each thread as before.

3 Take the two other wires and thread on a seed, a pearl, a seed, a gold crystal, a seed, a silver crystal, a seed, a gold crystal, a seed, a pearl, and a seed. Pass the two left-hand threads through a hematite crystal, and then pass the right-hand threads through.

4 Cross both sets of thread through a 5mm bead passing the right-hand threads to the left and the left-hand threads to the right.

5 On each double set of wires, thread on a hematite crystal, a seed, a silver crystal, and a seed. Cross both sets of thread through a 5mm round bead as shown in step 4.

6 Taking each of the four strands separately, choose one from the left and one from the right, which will go into the central two holes of the clasp. Thread on a seed, a gold crystal, a tubular crimp, and a seed on each. Then thread these wires into the central holes. Pass the wire back down through the beads, and crush the crimp with flat-nosed pliers as described in basic techniques. Trim the wire ends.

7 On the two remaining strands thread a seed, a crystal, a seed, a crimp, and a seed, and pass the right wire through the right hole of the clasp, and the left wire through the left hole. Pass the wires back down through the beads, and crush the crimp with flat-nosed pliers as described in basic techniques. Trim the wire ends. Repeat from the beginning to create the other side.

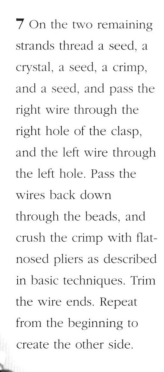

Starry Faux Lariat

The owner of my favorite bead store is obsessed with stars. Every time I go in,
there's a new star bead she's found and is intent on showing me.
So, with a little pile of shooting stars beside me, I threaded more and more
onto different strands, and suddenly there was a starry necklace. But something
was still missing, the stars didn't seem to shoot, just hang, so I added a couple
of long strands that could be tied to let the stars speed downward.
This style of necklace—a long strand of beads that is knotted casually
at the front—is called a lariat. This one is a fake because it has a clasp at the back.

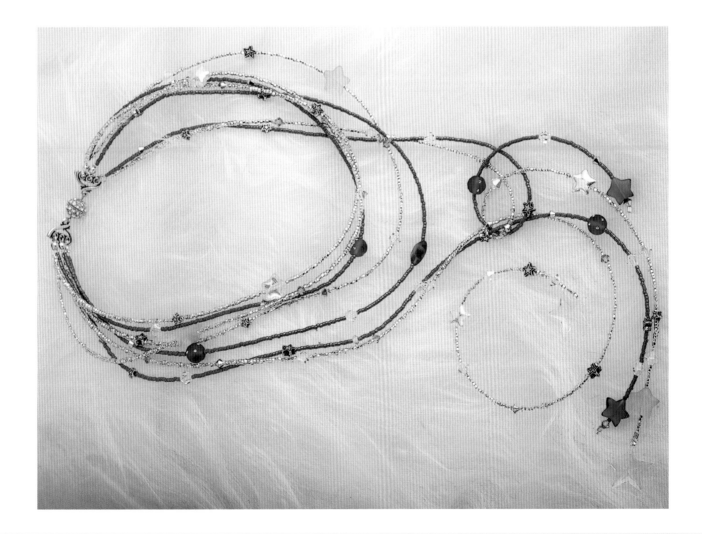

Materials:

Diamanté ball clasp
Two three-to-one necklace findings
Six silver necklace ends
16 silver crimps
0.5mm nylon beading wire in lengths of two x
20", two x 24", 16", 16½", 17", 17½", 18"
Two crystal stars
½ ounce of silver seeds
¼ ounce of blue Delicas
Five blue and diamanté round beads
Three white frosted stars
Three blue frosted stars
Four iridescent stars
21 x 5mm crystals
Five 4mm blue crystals
12 4mm silver crystals
10 tiny silver stars
11 small silver stars

Equipment:

Flat-nosed pliers
Round-nosed pliers
Wire cutters

Instructions

1 Thread three shortest lengths of wire through a necklace end, and secure with a crimp. Repeat for the 17½" and the 18" wires. Combine one 20" length with one 24" length; secure with crimp. Repeat with the other 20" and 24" lengths.

2 Start threading silver seed beads on the shortest length first—include one of the iridescent stars and a few tiny and small stars randomly spaced with seeds all the way down the length.

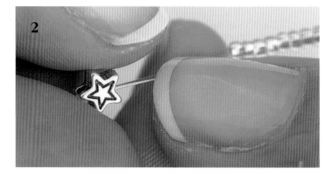

3 Stop threading about 1" from the end of the wire; place a crimp on the very end of the wire; and crush. This is just to hold the beads on the wire while you thread up the others.

4 Thread the next wire with blue Delicas, and include a round bead and a few crystals. The third strand is silver with two iridescent stars and a few crystals. The fourth strand is silver and includes a

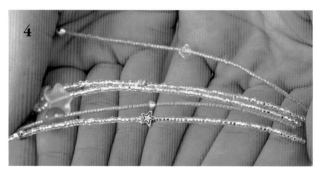

frosted star, crystals, and small silver stars. The fifth is blue with a blue frosted star, a blue round bead, and a few little stars and crystals. Place a crimp on the end of each strand, 1" from the end.

5 Thread the remaining long four strands with one blue and one silver strand on each piece. Use all the remaining small stars and crystals, making the lengths of seeds between large beads less and less. When you reach about 1" from the bottom of the silver strand, thread two seeds, a tubular crimp, and two seeds, then a crystal star and two seeds. Thread the end of the nylon wire up through the crimp and a few seeds. Pull tight, and crush the crimp. Trim the nylon wire.

6 On the blue strands finish with a frosted blue star, a Delica, and a crystal. Thread on a tubular crimp and crush.

7 Attach the three-to-one findings to both sides of the clasp, and then attach the necklace ends to the finding, including the five short lengths and one of the long two-strand components.

8 Gather the crimped ends of the three shortest strands, and very carefully snip off the crimp. Thread them through a necklace end, and re-crimp. Close the necklace end around them, and attach to the second three-to-one component. Repeat for the next two lengths, and attach the other long length.

Wire Work

Wire work is a very ancient art, indeed. The Celts used twisted metal wire to cover their torques, and made jewelry chains from fine wire loops. As well as being used for all the component findings, many cultures also use wire to decorate their beads—Bali silver work and Chinese cloisonné beads are but two. In modern times, some enterprising designers have used wire for amazing knitting and crochet projects that include beads within the forms created. Just like beads, wire comes in so many different metals and beautiful colors; I just have to have a skein in every color and thickness.

Making intricate jewelry from wire is a very satisfying way to spend a summer evening, and for all these interesting projects you do not even need to be able to solder pieces together. Smart wire work looks classy, and once you've mastered the basic techniques, you can amaze your friends with your professional finishes and calm efficiency. Take your time to get these techniques right. Holding the pliers will feel strange at first, but go slow and try to keep loops as small as possible, the wraps as tight as possible, and always trim spare wire flush with the work so that you don't get scratched!

Sterling-silver wire is wonderful for special projects, but if you're feeling frugal, silver- or gold-plated is much cheaper and just as pretty. You can even buy it already twisted. Silver wire will tarnish over time, and intricate wire projects can be hard to clean or polish, so to make sure your work remains shiny: keep it wrapped in acid-free tissue somewhere dark, such as a jewelry box.

Some people are allergic to certain metals, so always be aware of any problems that the eventual owner of your creation may have—nickel is a particularly common allergy irritant.

Wire comes in various gauges; I find 0.4mm to be the most useful for my work. It is both strong but still fairly flexible. Very thick wire can be stiff and hard to work, although softer versions of thick wire that bend easily can be found if you look. However, these soft wires don't hold their shapes as well, so they aren't always the best option. Very fine wire can be prone to snapping, just as any thin thread might and it will break if you overwork it. If you try not to bend a piece in the same place over and over again then you should avoid any trouble.

Tools used for wire work may be

Left: Glass beads with fancy spiral headpins

Above: Wrapped loops with pressed-glass beads
Right: Beads with wire embellishments

coated with a rubberized sealant to prevent getting marks and scratches on the pieces while they are being shaped. It's very easy to use: just dip in the open plier tips, and let it dry. It provides a thin barrier between the two metals that assists grip but doesn't enlarge the size of the plier jaw too much. I think it is a great investment.

Large wire shapes may also be hammered flat with a small hammer on a hard surface to create a lovely patterned texture.

If you enjoy working with wire and want to create more intricate shapes, you may want to invest in a wire jig, which has many tiny holes into which pegs are inserted to create different patterns. You can wrap the wire around the pegs to create a variety of exciting shapes and perfect curves. There are big and little jigs, and jigs for making spirals. There are some very cheap ones available but the more expensive ones tend to be sturdier with metal pegs that make using them much easier. If you need to make a matching pair of components for earrings, you will find a jig invaluable.

If you are caught without a suitable clasp for a project, you can always fashion one of your own based around the classic S-shaped design. You can even include one of the beads from the necklace within the form of the S. This also gives you the opportunity to make unique colorful clasps that may not be available to buy. You can also try creating your own headpins with a fancy end—a spiral or heart looks very sweet.

You can even make your own beads from twisted wire or wire wrapped around a larger gauge and then rolled around a pencil or piece of dowel. You can freeform with wire successfully too, wrapping and weaving it around a bead or into a shape, inserting beads as you go for some very exciting solid bracelets or pendants.

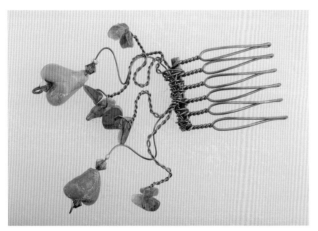

All pictures: A collection of wire beading projects

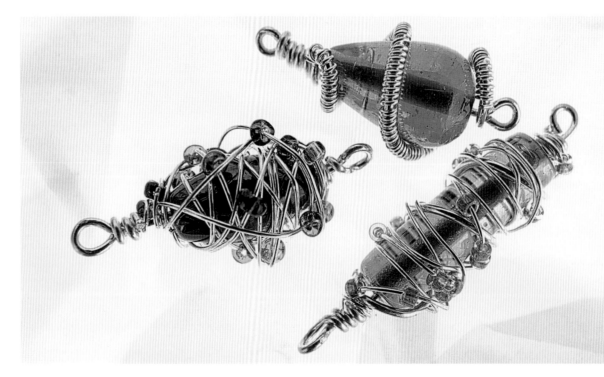

Basic Wire Techniques

Headpin loop

1 Grip the round-nosed pliers about 1" from the top of the wire.

2 Twist the pliers through 90 degrees away from you, creating a right angle.

3 With your free hand curve the top piece of wire back toward you, shaping it tightly over the top of the pliers.

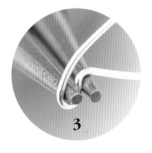

4 Keep curving until it crosses the other piece of wire; remove the round-nosed pliers.

5 Slide the wire cutters inside the loop so the cutting edge is flush with the inside edge of the wire circle, and snip.

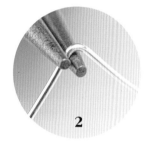

Wrapped loop

1 Grip the round-nosed pliers about 1" from the top of the wire.

2 Twist the pliers through 90 degrees away from you, creating a right angle.

3 With your free hand, curve the top piece of wire back toward you, shaping it tightly over the top of the pliers.

4 Keep curving until it crosses the other piece of wire; remove the round-nosed pliers.

1

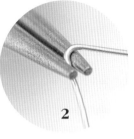
2

3

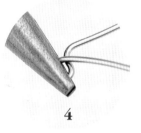
4

5 Grip the loop in flat-nosed pliers.

6 Start wrapping the tail around the stem wire neatly.

7 Wrap three times close together; then snip close to the stem.

5

6

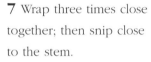
7

7

Opening and closing jump ring

1 Hold each side of the ring with pliers, and twist. Do not pull apart, or it will not return to a perfect circle.

2 To close, grip each side with pliers and twist back again.

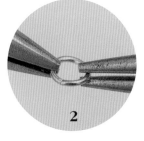

Surgeon's knot (for two ends)

1 Cross the left-hand thread over the right-hand thread, and wrap right around.

2 Now cross the right-hand thread over the left-hand thread, and pull up through the hole.

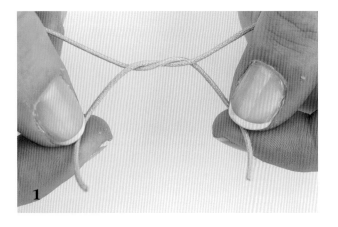

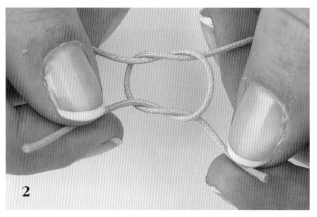

3 Wrap underneath, and pull up through the hole again.

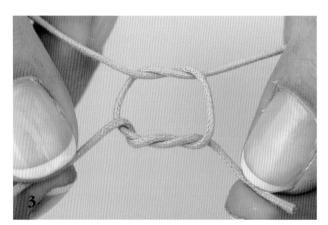

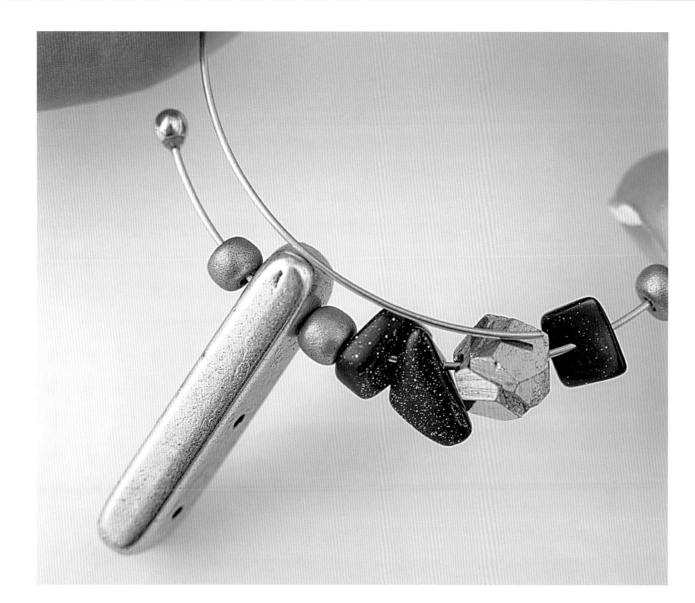

Necklace ends

1 To close a crimp, hold it between the jaws of a pair of flat-nosed pliers and squeeze until it is flat.

OR

2 Tie a large knot or even two or three, and then trim the ends.

Thread on a necklace end, and close gently around the crimp or knot.

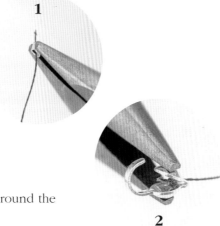

Vintage-Style Chandelier Earrings

This antique type of finding can be very useful for all sorts of projects. Although the findings have a Victorian style, I think that these long earrings have a baroque, almost gypsy look to them. Their rich medieval colors suit the dark wire work admirably, and I love the deep red and purple together as it just looks so regal. Why not incorporate your birth stones with a choice of crystals or add beads to match your new colors. You could even try some colored wire for a brighter and more contemporary style.

Materials:

Two three-to-one vintage-style necklace ends
Two black fish hooks
Six black headpins
12 x 2" lengths of 4mm black wire
Six 6mm crystals
Six 4mm crystals
Six tumble chips
Six 4mm fire-polished beads
Two 6mm pearls
24 x size 9 seed beads
10 x size 6 seed beads

Equipment:

Flat-nosed pliers
Round-nosed pliers
Wire cutters

Instructions

1 Thread a size 9 seed, 4mm crystal, tumble chip, and a size 9 seed onto a headpin, and make a smart top loop. Wrap as described in basic techniques.

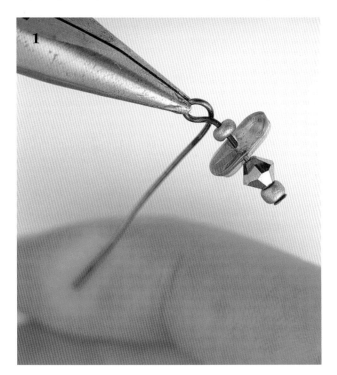

2 On one of the 2" pieces of wire, create a small loop about ¾" from the end. Thread this new loop through the previous wrapped loop, and wrap the new loop.

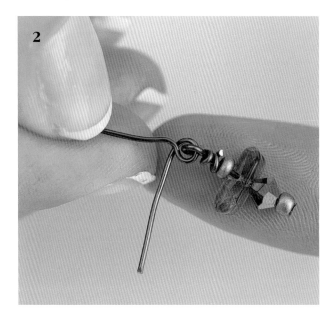

3 Next thread on a size 6 seed bead, a 6mm crystal, and a size 9 seed. Then make a top loop, and wrap neatly.

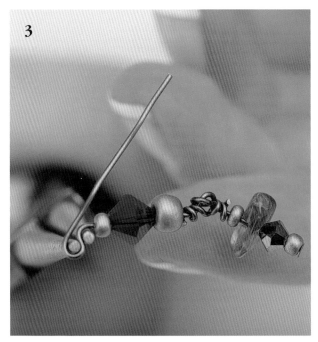

4 On another of the 2" pieces of wire, create a loop about ¾" from the end. Thread this wire through the previous loop, and wrap. Thread on a 9 seed, fire-polished, 9 seed, pearl, and 9 seed. Make a top loop, put this loop through center of finding; wrap.

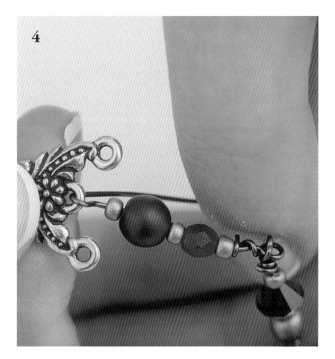

5 Then make the two sets of side pieces, placing the beads in this threading order:

- Bottom section: 6 seed, fire-polished, 9 seed.
- Middle section: 4mm crystal, tumble, 9 seed.
- Top section: 6 seed, 6mm crystal, 9 seed.

Attach these pieces on either side of the finding, using a loop and wrap as before. To attach the finding to the fish hook, twist open the loop, as you would a jump ring, and thread on the finding, twisting the loop to close.

Beaded Hoop Earrings

I have several friends who are well known for their fabulous, and usually huge, earrings. No matter what the occasion, they always seem to have a new and ever more exciting pair. So, not to be outdone, I created this opulent design that combines the always-popular hoop shape with long dangles for maximum effect. The colors within the cloisonné beads dictated the array of crystals and semiprecious chips, giving the final objects an overwhelming look of old Imperial Chinese textiles and embroideries.

Materials:

Four round cloisonné beads
Two long oval cloisonné beads
Eight size 7 gold seeds
20 x 4mm turquoise crystals
Four 3mm magenta crystals
Eight 5mm rose crystals
12 x 5mm green crystals
Four 4mm pink crystals
Eight citrine tumble chips
Four peridot tumble chips
Four 4mm lapis beads
Two 4mm jump rings
Two fish hooks
Two coils of small bracelet memory wire
Six headpins

Equipment:

Memory-wire cutters
Flat-nosed pliers
Round-nosed pliers
Wire cutters

Instructions

1 Grip the very end of one piece of memory wire with a pair of round-nosed pliers, and curve it outward. It will be very stiff, but try and make a complete tiny round loop, with no gap. Place it to one side.

2 Then thread a crystal, cloisonné bead, and a crystal on each of the headpins, using eight turquoise and four green crystals. Make a neat top loop.

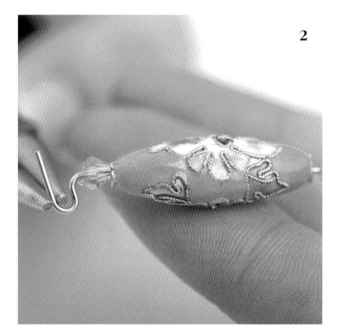

3 Thread on the rest of the beads to the memory wire loop in this order: turquoise, citrine, rose, magenta, rose, citrine, turquoise, green, gold, green, turquoise, and peridot. Then thread on a headpin with one of the round bead dangles.

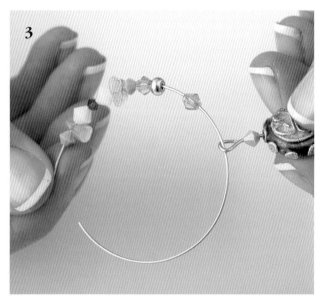

4 Thread on a lapis, gold, pink, and the central oval headpin dangle. Repeat the bead threading symmetrically on the other side. Leave ½" of wire showing. Snip off any excess, and then make another loop with the round-nosed pliers.

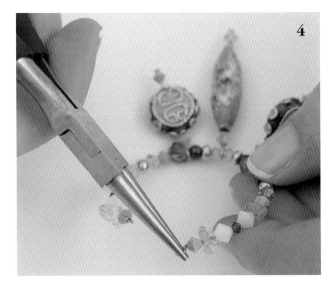

5 Open a jump ring as described in basic techniques, and thread through the loops from each side of memory wire. To finish it off, thread on a fish hook, and twist the jump ring to close. Make a second hoop in the same way for the other ear.

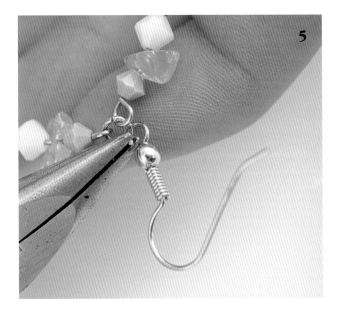

Night Sky Memory-Wire Bracelet

For those of us who like chunky jewelry, this cuff looks as though it has been made from meteorites and pieces of twinkling night sky. I think the overall effect is definitely out of this world! I love the combinations of big faceted stones, but the natural mineral of pyrite has a high amount of copper in it and so it should never be wet or it goes green. Blue goldstone is not a stone at all but is created from glass and sparkling dust. To keep it clean, just polish carefully with a soft dry cloth.

Materials:

Four large three-hole gold spacers
Six 6mm faceted blue goldstone
6" string of blue goldstone tumble chips
12 faceted chunks of pyrite
Three coils of large bracelet memory wire
Six memory-wire ends
½ ounce of gold size 6 beads

Equipment:

Epoxy glue
Tape
Memory-wire cutters

2 When the glue is completely set, thread on a gold bead, a spacer, and a gold bead. Then thread on two tumble chips, a pyrite piece, a chip, another gold bead, and a second spacer.

Instructions

1 Glue three of the memory ends to one end of each wire, using the mixed epoxy glue and a toothpick to apply. Don't worry if you get a tiny bulb of glue at the foot of the bead; it will dry clear. Leave it to dry according to the manufacturer's instructions.

3 Thread on about 2½" of assorted chips and beads, placing a gold bead either side of the 6mm faceted stones. Thread on a gold bead, a spacer, and a gold bead. Wrap a bit of tape on the end of the wire to hold the beads in place until the final cap can be glued on.

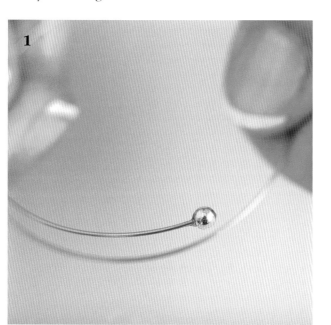

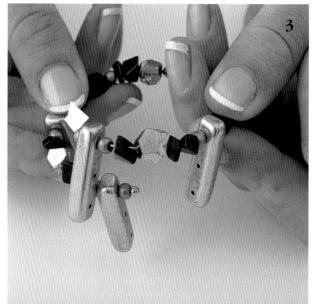

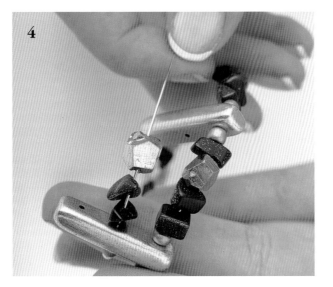

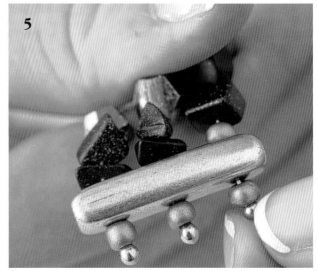

4 Repeat steps 2 and 3 for the second and third wires, threading them through the middle and bottom holes in the spacers. Make sure the length of stones between each spacer is exactly the same as the first—you may have to add or subtract beads because they are all irregular shapes and sizes.

5 Snip off any excess memory wire with the appropriate cutters, leaving ⅛" to glue into a memory-wire end. Be careful: you don't want all the beads to fall off. Glue the remaining three ends to the ends of each wire using the mixed epoxy glue and a toothpick. Leave to dry thoroughly.

Scarab Choker

*Whitby jet was the pinnacle of chic in Victorian times and occasionally you
can find fabulous jet beads in antique shops. They sparkle exquisitely from
hundreds of hand-cut facets and are just as strong as the day they were made. However,
the threads holding them together sometimes disintegrate. This choker is made with
all modern beads, but I feel it could very easily have been worn by Mina Harker as
she pursued Dracula along the cliff tops at Whitby. Egyptian artifacts were favorite
exotic motifs in Victorian times, but this necklace would look just as lovely with
a different art-bead centerpiece.*

Materials:

Scarab bead
10 x 6mm black onyx beads
28 x 6mm matte black pearls
24 x 4mm jet crystals
14 x 6mm jet crystals
¼ ounce of small jet bugle beads
Black nylon bead wire
11 x 2" lengths of 4mm black wire
Two necklace ends and two crimps

Equipment:

Flat-nosed pliers
Round-nosed pliers
Wire cutters
Scissors and glue

Instructions

1 Make a small wrapped loop on one of the 2" pieces of wire, as described in basic techniques. Thread on the scarab bead, and wrap and trim the other end. Repeat for all 10 of the black onyx beads to make the wire bead components.

2 Take a 5" length of nylon wire, and thread on one end of the scarab, a black onyx component, a 6mm crystal, onyx, 6mm matte bead, onyx, crystal, onyx, matte, onyx, crystal, onyx, other end of the scarab, crystal, and so on, repeating the pattern symmetrically. Tie the nylon wire in a surgeon's knot, and put a dot of glue on the knot. Trim.

3 Cut a 7" length of nylon wire, and starting at the top of the scarab, thread on the other end of the onyx component, then a 4mm crystal, a small bugle bead, a 6mm crystal, bugle, 4mm, onyx component end, 4mm, two bugles, 4mm, onyx, 4mm, two bugles, 6mm, two bugles, 4mm, onyx, and repeat symmetrically all around the inner circle. Tie the nylon wire in a surgeon's knot and put a dot of glue on the knot. Trim.

4 Cut two 20" lengths of nylon wire, and thread one around the outer circumference of beads through each one, along the side of the scarab. Pass one thread from the second onyx component to the fifth; thread another between the third and fourth.

6 Thread on a necklace end and a crimp, and crush the crimp with flat-nosed pliers. Trim the wires and close the necklace end as described in basic techniques. Attach one end of a clasp with round-nosed pliers, and repeat from step 4 on the other side.

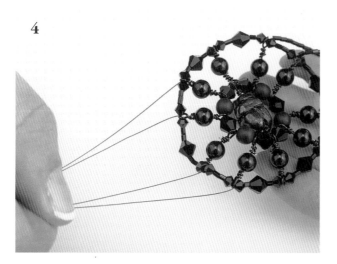

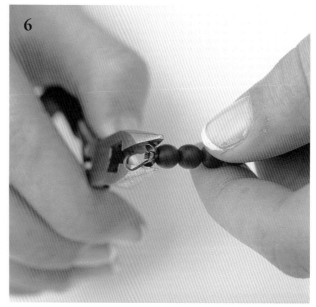

5 Thread on 2" of bugle beads to the outer two side threads and about 1¾" onto the inner thread. Adjust the numbers of beads until all four threads lie flat when joined to enter a 6mm crystal. Thread through all four wires a matte bead, 4mm crystal, a matte bead, 4mm crystal, and 10 matte beads.

Vintage-Style Rose Necklace

Roses were a popular motif among the romantic Victorians. Not content with merely growing them, Victorians carved roses from every available stone, including jet and coral. I am devoted to these coral roses and am often found desperately searching for them in antique shops. Because coral is now a protected substance in most parts of the world, these pink coral shapes are now very rare.

Fortunately there are lots of other nice pink and red materials from which to carve flowers. This gorgeous cluster of roses is made from oven-baked clay, so if you're feeling creative why not make your own? The rosebuds are fashioned from thin clay strips rolled up between the fingers, baked, then inserted into a sphere of soft clay and baked again.

Instructions

1 Thread the three headpins with the beads in the following sequences, and create a small loop at the top with the round-nosed pliers, as described in basic techniques.

- 4mm MOP, red seed, opal pellet, 4mm cream pearl, 5mm gold pearl.
- 5mm MOP, 5mm cream pearl, crystal, 4mm gold pearl, crystal, opal pellet, 4mm silver pearl.
- Teardrop, 5mm gold pearl, 4mm silver pearl, crystal.

2 Thread a 6mm cream pearl either side of the rose bead onto an eyepin, and create a loop at the top.

Materials:

One large rose-inspired bead
Three black headpins
33 x black eyepins
One black lobster clasp
Seven black jump rings
One 4mm gold pearl
10 x 5mm gold pearls
Six 6mm gold pearls
Two 4mm silver pearls
Six 5mm silver pearls
Three 6mm silver pearls
Three 4mm cream pearls
One 5mm cream pearls
Two 6mm cream pearls
Three 4mm mother of pearl
10 x 5mm mother of pearl
10 x 4mm crystals
Five opal pellets
One teardrop crystal
Two frosted, iridescent, red, size 5 seed beads

Equipment:

Flat-nosed pliers
Round-nosed pliers
Wire cutters

3 On a second eyepin thread a 4mm cream pearl, a red seed, and another 4mm pearl. Finish by making a loop. Twist one loop to open, and attach the rose component to one end and the three headpins to the other.

4 For the central triangle, make up these components on eyepins in the same manner as step 3.

- Two crystals, 5mm gold pearl, 5mm MOP, 5mm gold pearl, crystal.
- Two opal pellets, 6mm silver pearl, opal pellet.
- Two crystals, 6mm silver pearl, crystal.
- One 6mm gold pearl, 4mm MOP, 6mm silver pearl, 4mm MOP, 6mm gold pearl.

Attach them together with the jump rings or by twisting the eyepins together.

5 For the final chain, make up all these pieces on eyepins, making sure to keep the loops all the same size:

- Eight 5mm MOP
- Four 6mm gold pearls
- Six 5mm gold pearls
- Six 5mm silver pearls

Attach them together as before and add to the rest of the necklace. Finally, attach the clasp and a jump ring to the last mother of pearl eyepins by carefully twisting one jump ring open, adding the clasp and top end of necklace, and twisting back to shut. On the other side just add the jump ring. Attach the big rose to the bottom of the central triangle.

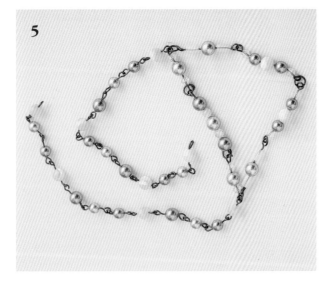

Leaf-and-Chain Earrings

Just before the leaves fall from the trees in Autumn, they seem to hang from the branches
by no more than a thread, falling with the slightest breeze. I wanted to re-create that
feeling of movement and fragility with these gorgeous iridescent beads and crystals.
Because these leaves hang from a fine chain, they move in a more fluid
way than ordinary headpin dangles and are light to wear.

Materials:

Six iridescent glass leafs
Six 4mm crystals
Six seed pearls
2" of large trace chain
Six 2" of 0.4mm silver wire
Two silver fish hooks

Equipment:

Flat-nosed pliers
Round-nosed pliers
Wire cutters

Instructions

1 Cut the chain into two lengths with eight complete loops in each length. Discard any extra chain. Place the two lengths to one side.

2 On one 2" piece of wire, create a right angle bend about ½" from the end, using the flat-nosed pliers.

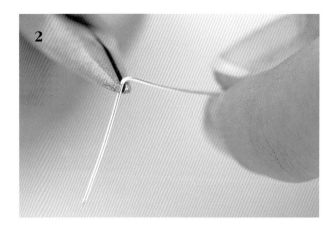

3 Thread on a glass leaf with the iridescent side facing the right-angle bend. Bend the wire gently behind the leaf with your fingers to cross just above the bead in a neat triangle. Snip off the excess with wire cutters, and slightly bend the long edge to lie straight upward using the flat-nosed pliers.

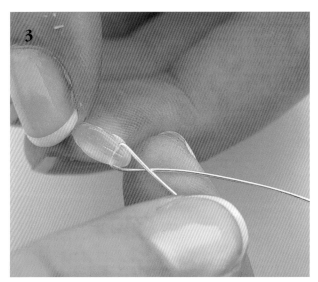

4 Thread on a crystal and a pearl and create a tiny loop ⅛" from the top of the pearl.

4

5

5 Thread the loop onto the bottom link of the chain, and wrap the loop very neatly as described in basic techniques.

6 Repeat from step 2, adding each dangle from alternate links of chain until you have three leafy dangles. Finally, attach the fish hook by attaching to the top link of the chain.

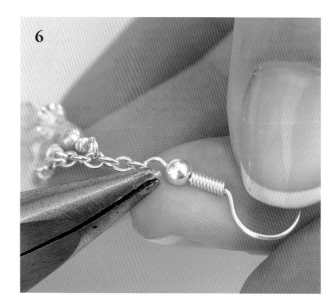

6

Feather Chandelier Earrings

One of my favorite trims is the huge feather hems seen on those amazing ballroom dancing dresses. I've always nurtured a secret passion for one, and Fred Astaire as a dance partner, of course! Delicate and yet dramatic, these dressy earrings combine freshwater pearls with ostrich feather drops and delicate wire work. Ostrich feather trim is usually sold by the inch or yard, although you can take a few strands from the bottom of a large plume if you prefer. The wired-flower technique could also be used to create a charming necklace, using the earring and feather drop as a central pendant.

Materials:

16 freshwater pearls
16 x 4mm fire-polished beads
Six 4mm jump rings
Two fish hooks
Two cord/feather ends
Two 3" of 0.4mm silver wire
Two 8" of 0.4mm silver wire
About 14 strands of ostrich feather

Equipment:

Flat-nosed pliers
Round-nosed pliers
Wire cutters
Glue

Instructions

1 Group seven strands of feather in one hand, and trim the top edges to neaten. Put a dab of glue inside the cord end, and push the feathers into it. Crush the cord end tightly around the feathers with flat-nosed pliers. Open and attach a jump ring to the top of the cord end.

2 Make a wrapped loop with a short piece of wire as described in basic techniques. Thread on two fire-polished, the feather component, and two fire-polished, and make another wrapped loop. Slightly curve this piece.

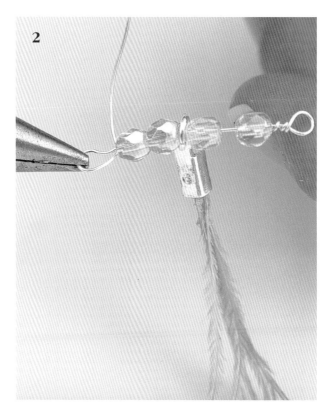

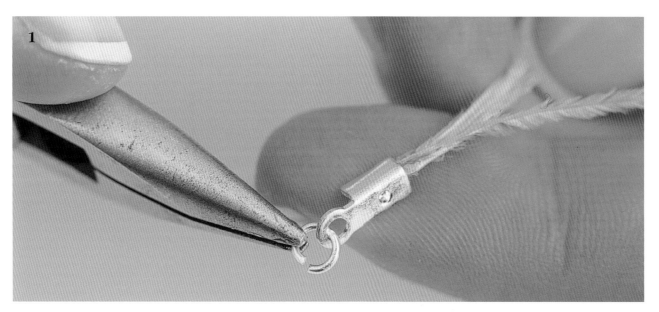

3 Make a wrapped loop at the end of an 8" piece of wire, thread on four pearls, curve around to create a loop, and wrap twice around the wrapped loop.

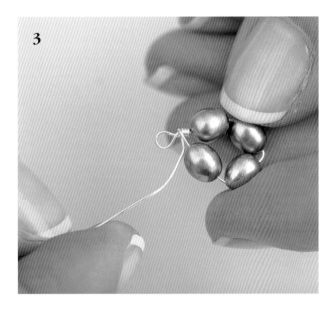

4 Thread on a fire-polished bead, and pass the wire through the pearl loop. Make a wrapped loop between pearls two and three.

5 Turn over the pearl circle, and thread on another fire-polished bead to the back. Wrap around the loop once more. Thread on four more pearls; make a circle and wrap at the top; then repeat the steps from step 4. Attach the long feather piece to each side of the pearl flowers with 4mm jump rings and attach the fish hook at the top.

Crystal Heart and Pearl Necklace

I love the sea, and I find myself instantly drawn to things that originated within the ocean's depths. All the delicious colors and shapes of shells available are amazing. If a country can have a national stone, then New Zealand's is the paua shell. It is the only place where paua, with its shining opalescent colors, is found. It comes from the shellfish of the abalone family and is gathered from the storm-swept beaches of the South Island. The pieces of iridescent shell are then cut and shaped into lovely shapes including stars, dolphins, and hearts. This pretty lightweight necklace could be worn by a mermaid or a surfer girl to remind you always of the ocean.

Materials:

1¾ coils of memory wire
Two memory-wire ends
Seven 2" lengths of 0.4 wire
Two headpins
Three ½" heart beads
Three crystal hearts
One 8mm crystal
Five 5mm crystals
Three 4mm crystals
Four 5mm pearls
120 4mm pearls
Two 6mm pearls

Equipment:

Memory-wire cutters
Glue
Flat-nosed pliers
Round-nosed pliers
Wire cutters

Instructions

1 Glue the end onto the memory wire with an epoxy glue; leave it to set until completely solid.

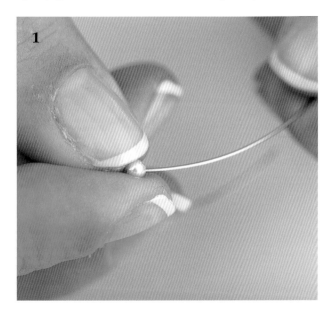

2 To create the center dangle, make a sharp bend in the wire with the flat-nosed pliers, leaving one ¾" end. Thread the crystal heart on the long end, and very gently make another bend with the pliers to create a U-shape. With your fingers, bend the long end forward to cross the other wire. If you are too heavy-handed you will crack the crystal, so be careful.

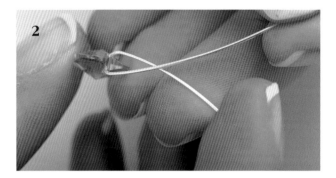

3 Hold the triangle with one pair of pliers, and with another, wrap the shorter end around the longer twice. Trim close to the stem.

4 Thread on a 5mm pearl; make a top loop; and wrap as described in basic techniques.

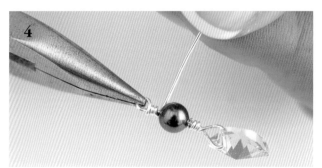

5 With another piece of wire, make a loop; thread through the previous loop; wrap; and add a 4mm crystal, a bead heart, and a 5mm crystal.

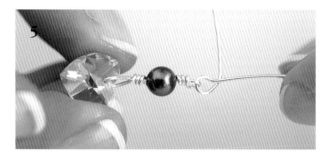

6 Make a loop, and wrap at the top of this second component. Add the top component in same way but using a 4mm pearl, an 8mm crystal, and a 4mm pearl. Finish with a top loop, and wrap.

7 Create the dangles on both sides in the same manner, but use only two components—the bottom one has a crystal heart and a 5mm pearl, and the upper has a 5mm crystal, 4mm pearl, 6mm pearl, 4mm pearl, and 5mm crystal.

8 Thread a bead heart, 4mm pearl, 4mm crystal, 4mm pearl, and 5mm pearl on each headpin, and make a wrapped loop at the top.

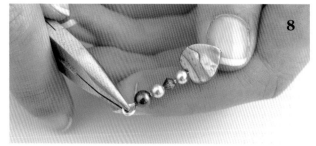

9 To actually create the necklace, thread on: 54 pearls, a headpin dangle, three pearls, a two-part dangle, three pearls, the center dangle, and then repeat the pattern symmetrically on the other side. Snip off any extra memory wire, but leave ¼" to glue the other end piece in place.

Beaded Flower Hairpins

*While looking at some antique couture gowns one day, I noticed one had
an adorable corsage of beaded flowers, still sparkling in perfect colors long
after the dress had faded. Upon investigation, I discovered this technique is called
"French beading," and flowers made in this way were a popular type of trimming
on hats and gowns in Victorian times. Some examples I have seen are absolutely
enormous, about a foot across, and weigh a lot for a hat trim.*

*In contrast to those gargantuan projects, these tiny flowers would
look fabulous scattered throughout a swept-up hairstyle. Although very time
consuming, in the hands of an experienced artist and using a variety of techniques,
just about any flower can be reproduced from seed beads and wire.*

Materials:

2 yards of 0.4mm wire
6" of 0.3mm green wire
¼ ounce of frosted size 10 seeds
¼ ounce of color-lined size 10 seeds
¼ ounce of green seeds
Three 4mm yellow crystals

Equipment:

Flat-nosed pliers
Wire cutters

Instructions

1 Thread seven frosted seeds onto an 8" length of wire, and twist together a couple of times to secure in a loop.

2 Thread seven more; twist, leaving a ¼" gap; and repeat until you have four flower petals.

3 Thread five frosted seeds, four color seeds, and five frosted seeds, and wrap around the last loops stem to create the second layer of the petal. Repeat for each of the four petals.

4 Loop the end of the wire back down through the first petal to secure them in a round. Thread on a yellow crystal, and place it in the center of the petals to make the middle of the flower. Pass the wire over the petals, and wrap till secure. Make two more complete flowers in exactly the same way.

5 To create the leaves, cut 6" of wire and thread on eleven seeds. Twist to secure for ¼". Add 11 more seeds on one wire, and twist curve into a loop ¼" from the other and twist. Repeat, and then twist wires all the way to the bottom.

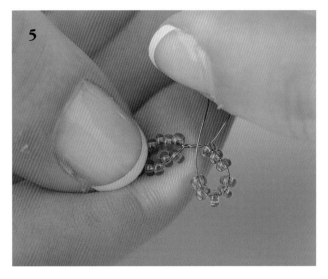

6 To assemble the bunch, hold all three flowers and the leaf branch and wrap the stalk pieces tightly with wire. Hold against the hairpins, and wrap wire around until secure.

Dragonfly Pin

Along the river bank I often see the enormous fairy-like wings of the dragonflies darting around. Their wings' opalescent transparency can be mimicked easily in glass, as Art Nouveau artist René Lalique knew. His dragonflies were legendary, combining the mythology of the dragon in stylized bodies and enormous eyes defined in gold or silver with the delicate iridescent wings copied in glass or enamels. Other artists of the period also used dragonfly and butterfly imagery extensively, including Tiffany in his beautiful stained-glass work. The look is re-created here with the use of attractive colored beads.

Materials:

3 yards of 0.3mm wire
20" of 0.6mm wire
¼ ounce of seed beads
Six bugle beads
One 6mm faceted bead
Two size 7 seeds
Stick pin

Equipment:

Epoxy glue
Flat-nosed pliers
Round-nosed pliers
Wire cutters

Instructions

1 Cut 6" of 0.3mm wire, and thread the two size 7 beads. Thread one end of the wire back through the beads, creating a loop and pull tight.

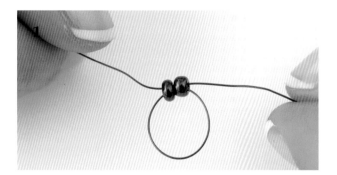

2 Thread the wire ends through the faceted bead, and then thread the six bugle beads.

3 Thread a seed bead on one wire, and pass the other wire through the bead the other way. Hold the wires in one hand, and twist the two ends together. Trim to 1" in length, and slightly curl this end with round-nosed pliers.

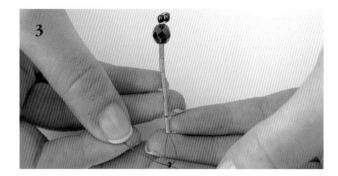

4 With the 0.6mm wire, create a loop of about 2" in length. Twist the ends, and make another loop on the other side. Wrap the wire around itself in the center, and make two more loops. Trim off any excess wire.

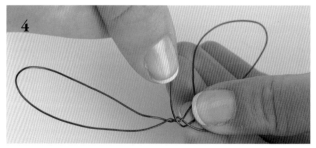

5 Place the body over the wing shape, and secure it by wrapping tightly just below the faceted bead with 0.3mm wire.

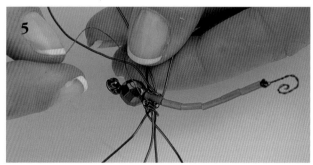

6 Cut a 20" length of 0.3mm wire, and secure it by wrapping around the wing case close to the body. Thread on two beads, and wrap the wire tightly around one wing with the beads pushed to the top and only wire on the underside.

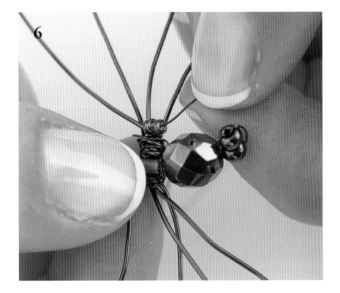

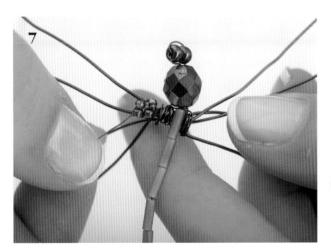

7 Hold the beads in place, and thread on two more. Continue wrapping seed beads all the way up the wing.

8 Occasionally wrap the wire around the 0.6mm wire a few times to secure; use different colored beads to create the wing spots.

At the tip of the wing, weave the wire on the back until all the beads are firmly held in place. Trim any excess wire, and repeat for the other three wings.

9 To make the dragonfly into a pin, glue it to the finding with epoxy glue, and leave it until it is completely set.

Looming

Using a loom to weave beads into long strips has its origins in Native American craft traditions. As they did not have written language, these people passed on ideas and messages by pictures and symbolic designs. Many of the designs were originally woven from only two colors of beads and these projects were made from wampum.

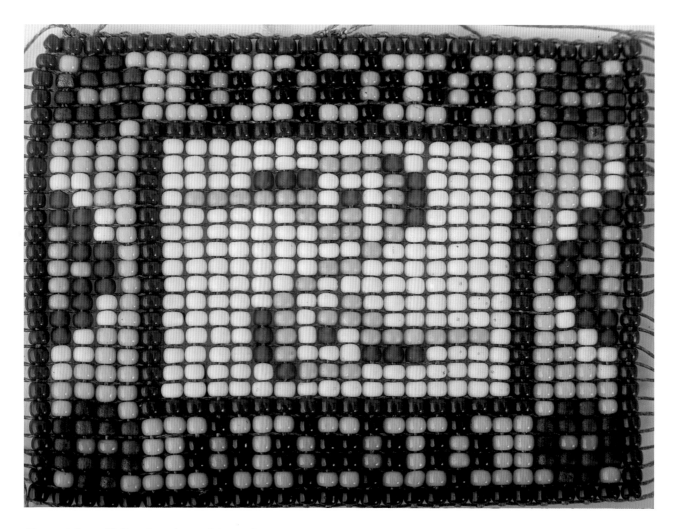

Above: A large Native American pictograph

Wampum beads, used in looming by the Native Americans, were small cylindrical beads made from the white and purple-black shell of the whelk and the quahog. These beads were cut and drilled by hand, a very time-consuming process, and were woven into belts and straps to record treaties, ceremonies, and stories.

Early looms were no more than a curved stick, like a bow. The threads were strung between each end with two slotted combs to hold the long warp threads apart. The beads were placed on the side-to-side weft thread and woven horizontally. Although looms have become more sophisticated, the method of weaving the beads has not changed for hundreds of years. The traditional patterns of each indigenous people continued as they reflected the world around them and their ancestral designs within the new bead work.

As the looming technique spread to other countries, new patterns and pictures were drawn in beads, using a rainbow palette instead of the favored red, turquoise, white, and black of traditional designs. A variety of warp threads—such as dyed linen, perle cotton, or satin cord—were also used to create a different look.

Looming produces a strong and neat piece of woven bead work. It is an easy technique to master—manufacturers of cheap bead looms often label their machines for ages seven and up, which shows how simple it actually is. It is a very swift method of creating bead cloth and has been rapidly adopted by bead artists all over the globe.

The use of Delica beads has reinvented the technique for many, and with their subtle palette and distinctive shape, they give a perfectly smooth finish. It is possible to create an almost photo-perfect rendition of a pictorial design using them.

Creating your own patterns is fun and easy with graph paper or one of the new pattern-creation computer programs designed specifically for bead work. Cross-stitch charts are also excellent, but remember to check how many colors you will need before getting too carried away. Beads of just one size should be used throughout—small

Above: Chunky glass pony beads in a bracelet

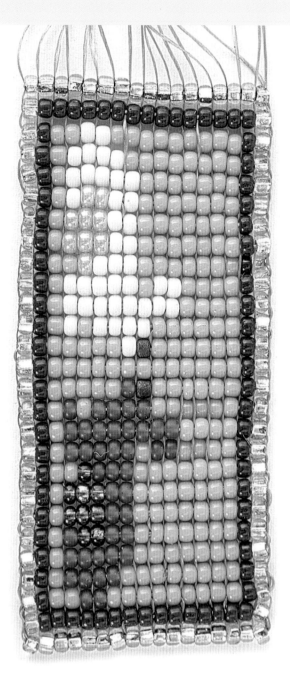

beads will obviously make a smaller picture, large beads a bigger one, but the size of bead doesn't make too much difference to the actual design proportions, so long as they are all the same size.

Many different types of looms are available from craft stores at very low cost. Alternatively, you may like to attempt making your own—there are great instructions available on the Internet if you feel adventurous. When choosing your loom, make sure you can weave the widest piece you may need in the future. You can always use fewer threads on a loom, but it's hard to add more if there's no space. But while a small loom does limit you to small pieces, it can be a good place to start for the beginner. Once you feel more confident, you can move on to a larger and more complex loom.

Looming is done with two sets of threads: warp threads are attached to the loom throughout the whole process; while the perpendicular weft thread is used for weaving, holding the beads, and wrapping around the warp thread. The type of thread required depends on the nature of the project—normal nylon thread is fine for basic beaded items, but for serious projects, a stronger thread might be needed for the warp. Always finish off both your warp and weft threads securely.

Left: A rabbit pictogram
Below: Delica beads form a lovely tight weave

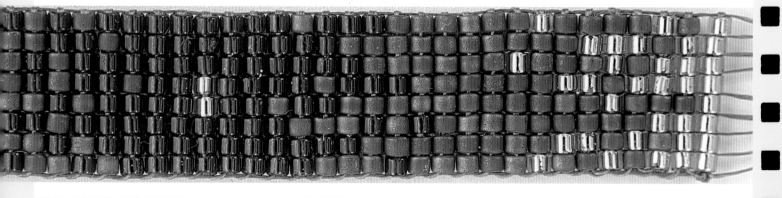

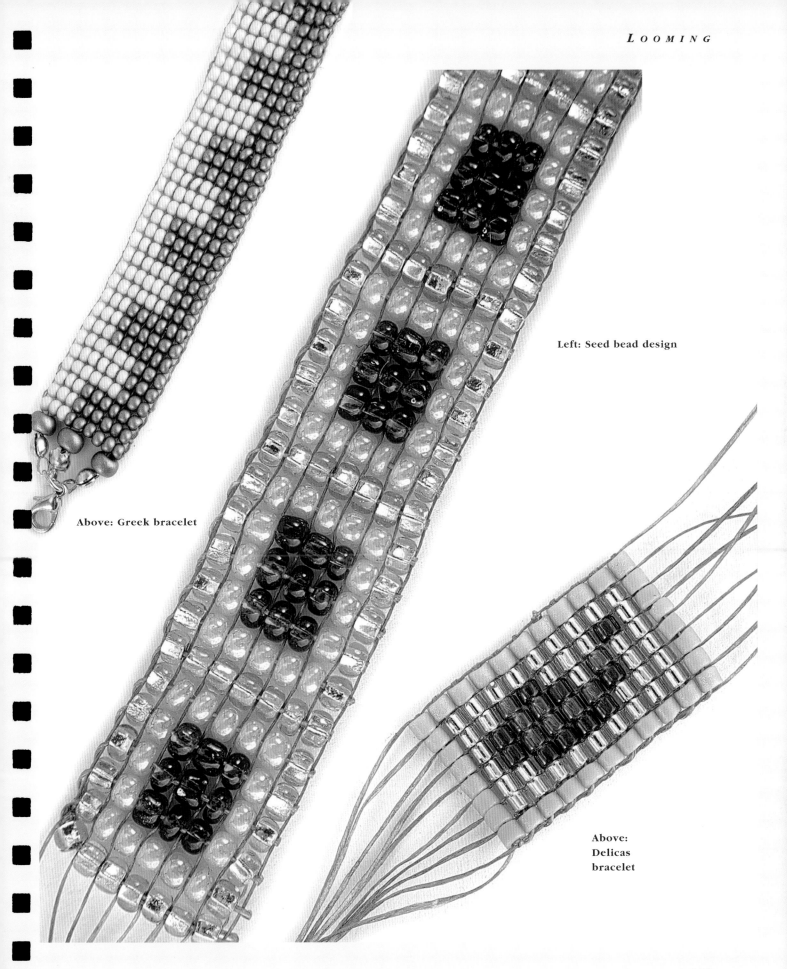

Left: Seed bead design

Above: Greek bracelet

Above:
Delicas
bracelet

103

Basic Loom Techniques

Setting up the bead loom

There are many different models of loom so refer to
your manufacturer's instructions for further details.

1 Tie one end
of your thread
through the
hole or to the
screw, or hook
on one side of
the loom.

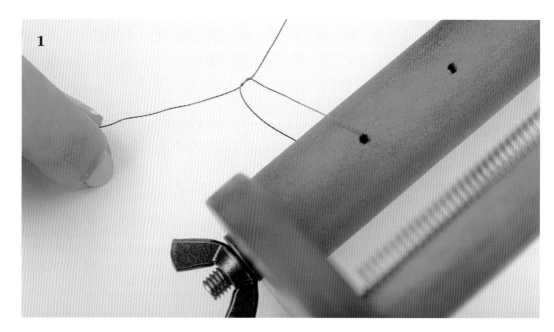

2 Pass the thread over the loom,
matching the gaps in the springs
or slots.

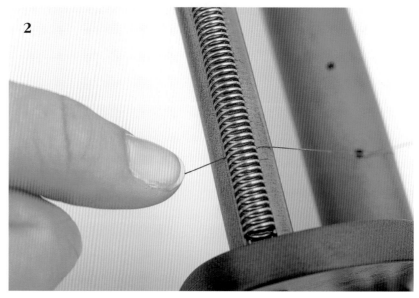

3 Wrap thread around the screw or hook on the other side, keeping the tension very firm.

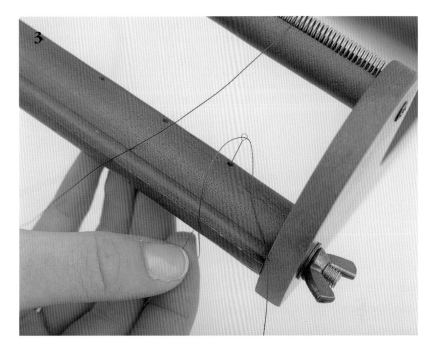

4 Pass the thread back over the loom, going between the next space in the spring or slots.

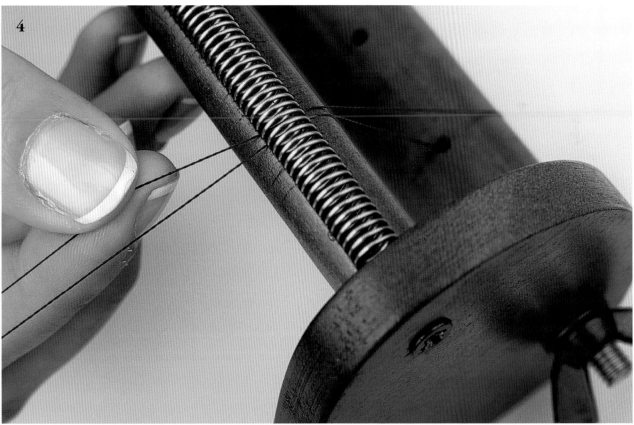

5 Continue until you have the correct quantity of threads, and tie off the last warp thread at the nearest hole, hook, or screw.

Starting thread and finishing off

1 To start off, tie the thread on to the left-hand outside warp with a secure knot. Leave a long tail.

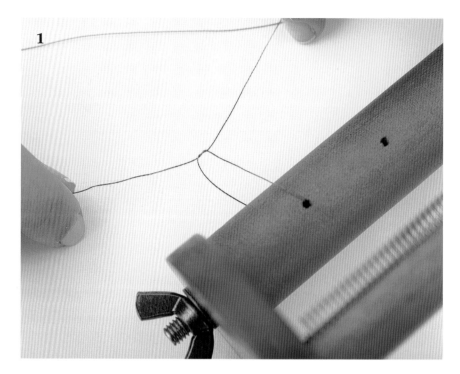

2 To finish, tie a knot around the warp; then pass the needle up through the line of beads. Pass the needle down the next row, up the next, then trim. Repeat with the tail from the start of the thread.

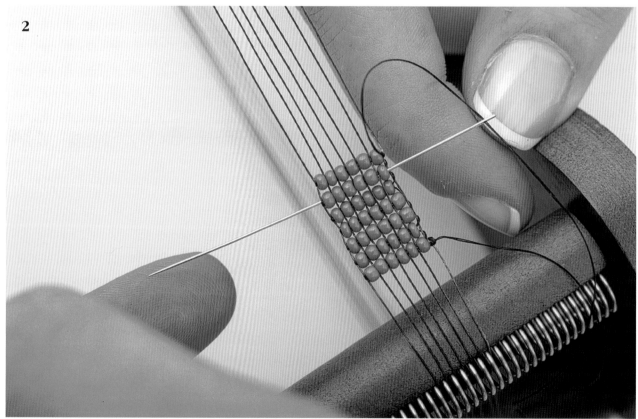

Basic weaving

1 Thread on all the beads in the first row of the pattern in order, reading from left to right. Pass the needle under the warp threads, placing the beads so each sits between two threads.

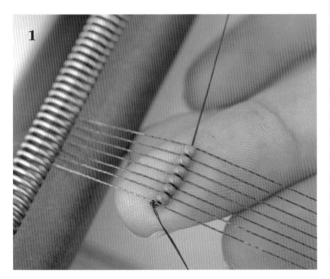

2 Support the beads carefully along your finger, and thread the needle back through the beads from right to left but passing the thread over the top of the warp threads. Pull the thread all the way through the beads.

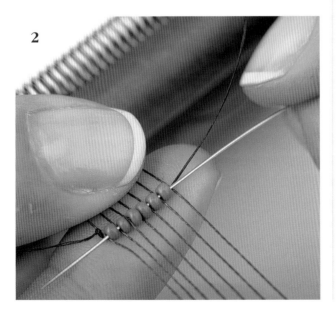

Adding thread

1 To add thread halfway through a project, weave the new tail back and forth through the loomed beads, exiting the last row in the proper direction for adding another line of beads.

Pre-Raphaelite Bracelet

This bracelet is inspired by some of the background flowers in Pre-Raphaelite artist William Morris's design **The Strawberry Thief***. William Morris was part of the Arts and Crafts movement in the late 19th century. His firm, Morris and Co., strived to provide objects of utility and beauty for the home, designing many beautiful and famous wallpapers and fabrics with which I could quite happily fill my interiors. The company, which originally included artists Edward Burne-Jones and Dante Gabriel Rossetti, was inspired by traditional medieval crafts, such as weaving and embroidery. It often used motifs from nature and heraldry to create its dense, swirling pictorial patterns.*

Materials:

¼ ounce of each color of size 11 seeds:

> Light green color lined
> Light green iridescent
> Mid green color lined
> Rust color lined
> Rust matte
> Purple/blue color lined
> Peach pearlized
> Red matte iridescent
> Red color lined

½ ounce of blue matte 11 seeds
18 x 4mm assorted green crystals
Four 4mm gold crystals
Three 4mm red/pink crystals
Perforated clasp finding
0.3mm wire
Strong nylon bead thread
Necklace ends

Equipment:

Sharp needle
Bead loom
Scissors and glue
Flat-nosed and round-nosed pliers

Pattern chart

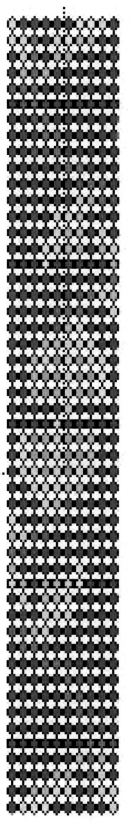

Light green color lined

Light green iridescent

Mid green color lined

Rust color lined

Rust matte

Purple/blue color lined

Peach pearlized

Red matte iridescent

Red color lined

Blue matte

Instructions

1 Thread up the bead loom with 10 strands of thread according to the instructions in basic techniques, and weave the pattern according to the chart. If the woven length seems too short, start the pattern again from the beginning and continue until the bracelet is long enough. Don't forget to leave a space for the clasp. Weave the weft ends in neatly to finish.

1

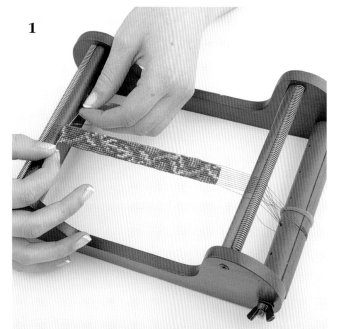

2 To make the clasp, cut a piece of wire about 10" long and thread one end 1" through the clasp. Place a crystal on the wire and thread the wire to the back of the clasp.

3 Thread the wire to the front of the clasp, and attach another crystal. Continue threading them on the clasp, using green ones around the outside and gold and red ones toward the center.

4 To finish, bring the wires to the back of the clasp, twist them together, and trim. Attach the clasp to its back plate by closing the catches with flat-nosed pliers.

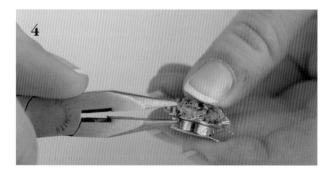

5 Cut the woven piece from the loom, leaving the threads long, and on one side, thread four seed beads to each of the threads. Divide them into two groups, and thread a necklace end to each group.

6 Tie a knot inside the necklace end, and put a dab of glue on the knot. Trim the spare thread, and close the necklace end. Repeat for the other group and all threads on the other side. Attach the necklace ends to each piece of the clasp using the round-nosed pliers.

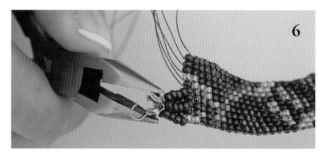

Loomed Swarovski Bracelet

Looming doesn't have to be only about seed beads. Any beads can be used for weaving on a loom so long as they are all the same size. These crystals come in such a perfect rainbow of colors I couldn't resist creating my own bow of faceted sparkle. This geometric design is quite modern in look but owes its inspiration very much to Art Deco.

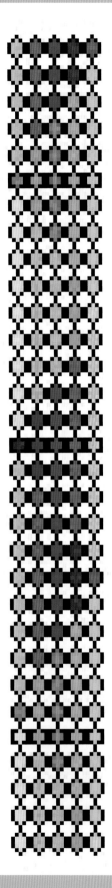

Pattern chart

Rose

Fuchsia

Ruby

Siam

Light siam

Ocean green

Indicolite

Emerald

Erinite

Peridot

Peach

Light peach

Light rose

Amethyst

Lavender

Capri blue

Sapphire

Light sapphire

Topaz

Smokey topaz

Materials:

20 crystals of each
color: rose, fuchsia,
ruby, siam, light
siam, ocean green,
indicolite, emerald,
erinite, peridot, light
peach, smoky topaz,
topaz, peach, light
rose, amethyst,
lavender, capri blue,
sapphire, and light
sapphire.
½ ounce size 11 silver
seeds
Strong nylon thread
T-bar clasp
Two rondelles
Two necklace ends

Equipment:

Sharp needle
Bead loom
Scissors and glue
Flat-nosed pliers
Round-nosed pliers

Instructions

1 Cut 4½ yards of thread
and thread one end onto a
needle. Thread up the bead
loom as described in basic
techniques. As you do so,
however, thread 30 silver
seeds onto each warp thread,
continuing until you have six
warp threads. Position the
beads within the top
weaving area.

2 Push a seed bead from each thread to the top of the loom, and secure your weft thread below them, on the left-hand thread.

3 Thread on the crystals from the first row of the pattern chart, and secure by weaving the needle back, as described in basic techniques. Push up another row of seed beads, and thread the needle down through the left-hand one.

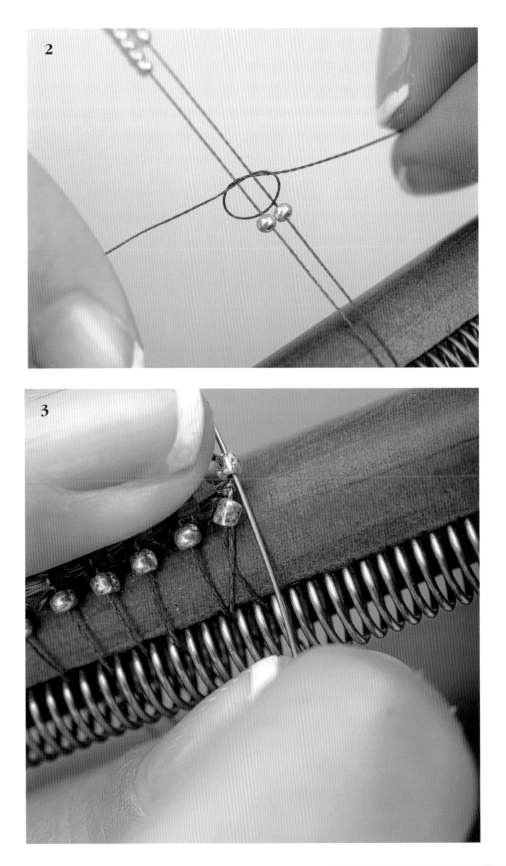

4 Continue threading crystals and pushing up rows of seeds, following the pattern chart. When the design is complete, secure the weft thread with a knot and by weaving it back through the work.

5 Remove your work from the loom by cutting the threads carefully, leaving equally long weft threads on each side.

6 On one side of the work, thread five seeds onto each weft thread, and using a wire needle, thread them all through a rondelle and a necklace end. Tie them securely with a square knot, and put a dab of glue on the knot.

7 Close the necklace end with flat-nosed pliers, and fasten on one end of the clasp with the round-nosed pliers. On other side, attach the other part of clasp.

Bead Woven Choker

This style of bone choker is almost synonymous with handcrafted jewelry. Originally, different motifs or large beads, quill rosettes, or feathers were placed in the center of the piece. I decided to use a bead-loomed motif representing two hummingbirds. The hummingbird was representative of both a clever homemaker and a small but spirited fighter in traditional designs. It is usually seen as a double design because the hummingbird is one of a faithful pair. You could even design and weave your own special centerpiece, but if you do, keep it to the same dimensions as mine or the rest of the choker won't work.

Pattern chart

Cream

Cobalt

Pearl turquoise

Green

Kingfisher blue

Dark frosted blue

Materials:

Six 2" bone tubes
Six 1" bone tubes
20 x 6mm round lapis beads
16 x 6mm round crystals
72 cylinder turquoise chips
Two large three/five hole spacers
Six silver necklace ends
¼ ounce of size 11 seeds in cream, cobalt, pearl turquoise, kingfisher blue, dark frosted blue, and green
Strong bead thread
T-bar clasp

Equipment:

Bead loom
Sharp needle
Scissors and glue
Wire needles
Round-nosed pliers

Instructions

1 Set up the loom with 18 threads as described in basic techniques, and weave up the pattern using the chart as a guide. Finish off the threads carefully and neatly.

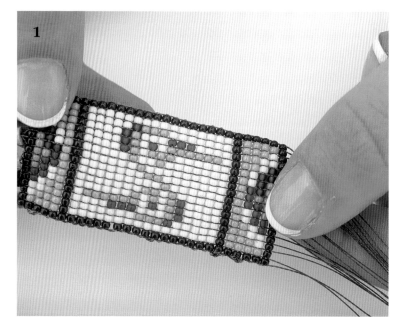

2 Next, cut the threads on the underside of the loom so that there are equally long lengths on each side of the woven piece.

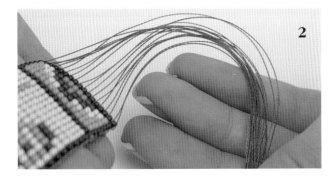

3 Place the woven piece flat in front of you, and thread a wire needle with the top right three threads; thread on a turquoise cylinder, a crystal, and another cylinder. Thread the next three threads with a second wire needle, and repeat.

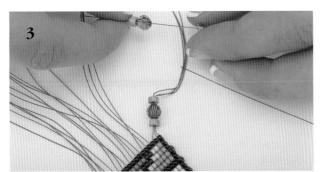

4 Then thread both needles through one of the 2" bone beads. On the top needle, thread on a cylinder, a lapis bead, and a cylinder. Pass it through the top hole of the spacer; thread on a cylinder, a lapis bead, and another cylinder. Repeat with the second needle.

5 Pass both needles through a 1" bone pipe and then through a necklace end. Tie the two groups of threads together with a square knot. Put a dab of glue on the knot; trim; and close the necklace end.

6 Repeat from step 3 for the all threads, but reverse the lapis and crystal beads.

7 Attach the necklace ends to the clasp using round-nosed pliers.

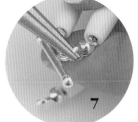

Embroidery

Beaded gowns and accessories have always been popular but were once only available to the very wealthy. Never before in the entire history of fashion has such intricately embroidered and beaded fabric been available at such affordable prices. We are fortunate to live in an age when machines are the predominant source of commercial embroidery. Less than a hundred years ago, all embroidery including beads, sequins, and gold threads had to be applied by hand. This job usually fell to highly skilled but poorly paid women who often worked a 14-hour day in bad light.

Above: Vintage jet beaded motifs

In 1770, a manual on embroidery including beading techniques was published by court favorite Charles de saint Aubin. I was amazed to learn that in some workshops embroiderers were trained to be ambidextrous, so that when they sat opposite each other at a table, they could both work from the light of the window without the shadow of their hands falling over the work. I can't imagine how hard it must have been to work with the wrong hand. He writes in great detail of many techniques, tips, and procedures, most of which are still relevant today in the big couture fashion houses.

When embroidering fabric, mainly small seeds and bugles were used with larger faceted stones and sequins for focus. Each and every bead had to be stitched on individually using back stitch or couching until a process called *tambour beading* was introduced. This type of embroidery uses a long fine hook similar to the ones used in crochet to create a chain stitch along the fabric, into which the pre-strung beads are secured. It was up to six times faster than previous methods and allowed for dresses to be completely covered in beads and sequins like exotic scales, as seen in 1920s designs.

It is believed that the tambour hook originated in India, and this is the method still used on many imported commercial garments because it is very speedy, once you know what you're doing. I am not at all speedy, definitely more tortoise than hare. Of course, if you break one thread then the whole chain of beading will unravel, just like knitting, cascading beads across the floor. For this reason most couture beading is still done by needle and thread.

Sequins are favorites to use in conjunction with seed beads in intricate embroidery, particularly bridal gowns and veils. Sequins are shaped flat disks punched from metal or, more commonly nowadays, plastic. They have a most particular type of reflective sparkle, covering a larger area than a bead, but they are much lighter in weight. They may be attached by thread using a seed bead in the center like a stopper bead to secure it. The popularity of novelty shapes was enormous in the 18th century and, even today, hundreds of different shapes are still available including leafs, stars, animals, and hearts.

An embroidery hoop will make working on fabric much easier. It holds the work taut, allowing the thread tension to be constant and the needle placement precise. They can be bought in both large and small sizes and round or square. Embroidery is usually done on the flat fabric pieces stretched in the frame before the article is constructed. There are times when this is not practical, such as if an edging design is to continue over a garment's seam or if you want to embellish a bought item. So be careful to keep the tension correct and, if the object has a lining, try not to catch it in the stitches.

Thread for attaching beads to fabric should be strong but fine. Sewing thread or fine beading thread are both good, and some specialty threads are available, too. A fine sharp needle is essential—it should go through the smallest beads with ease and be long enough to hold several beads if you intend to use couching. You should use a thread that is the same color as your material, not your beads. The beads themselves should be high quality with no sharp edges around the hole which could cut the fine thread.

Design inspiration can come from many sources; I often look at scraps of wallpaper and fabric for initial inspirations. Draw these out as pictures, then work out the lines of beading from these initial ideas. Transferring the design to the fabric can be freehand using a dressmakers' pencil or by tracing through dressmakers' carbon with a pin wheel.

The realm of the bead embroiderer is very large, so for inspiration you may also like to look at the incredible beaded gowns of Queen Elizabeth seen in her state portraits, the amazing 1920s beaded gowns of Erté, or the modern designer Thierry Mugler.

Patterned fabric can be embroidered directly over its existing shapes for extra depth and texture. Don't overstretch on your first projects, embroidery can be time consuming. Take time to experiment with ideas on small squares, then maybe use your experimental pieces to create a sampler cushion.

Below: Beaded tassel
Right: A selection of embroidered projects

Basic Embroidery Techniques

Starting thread

1 Make a couple of tiny stitches through the fabric, on top of each other, exactly underneath where your first bead is to be placed.

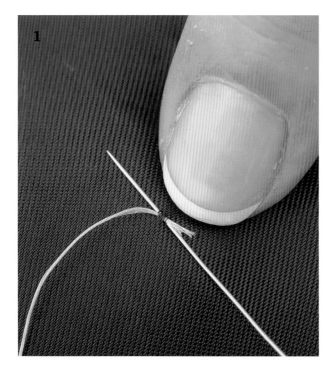

Finishing thread

1 Bring the thread to the back of the work and take a couple of tiny stitches through the fabric, on top of each other, exactly underneath where your last bead has been sewn on.

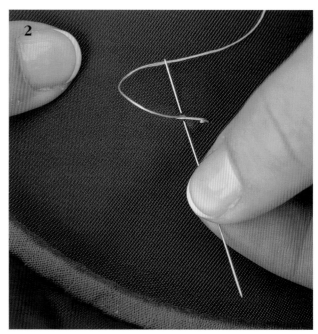

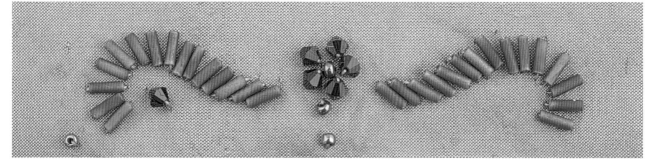

To couch beads

1 You will need two sharp needles and thread. Secure both threads to the material and thread on the beads.

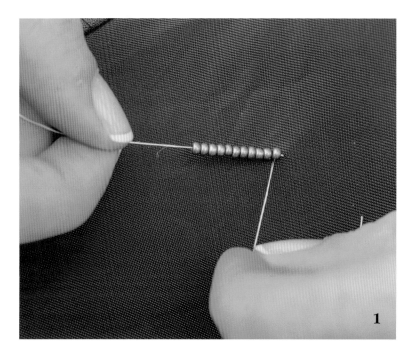

2 With the second needle and thread, start tying down every third or fourth bead by passing the needle over the beaded thread to a spot directly opposite and making a stitch.

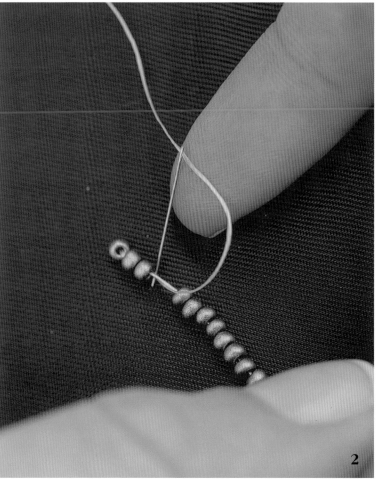

Beaded back stitch

1 Attach thread securely using a sharp beading needle. Place a bead on the needle, and push down to the fabric.

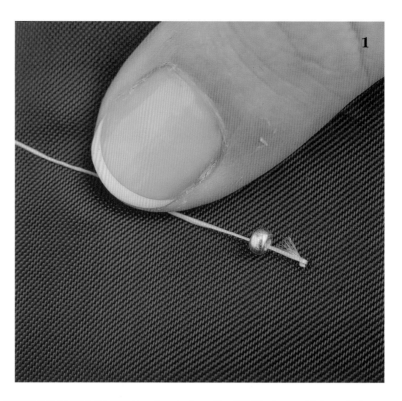

2 Make a backstitch, bringing the needle point up where you want the next bead to be. Add a bead, and repeat the back stitch. You can place the beads as close or far apart as you wish.

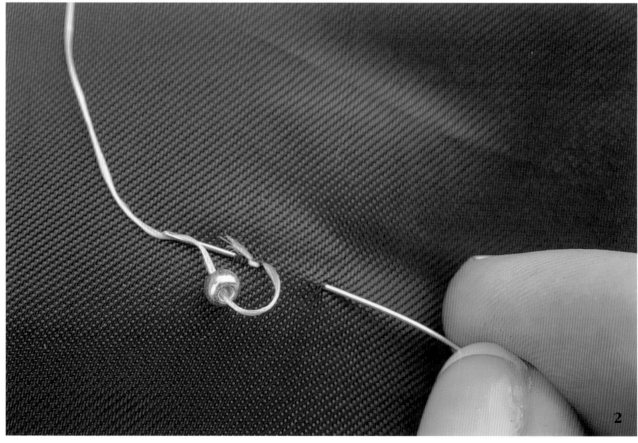

Fringing

1 Thread a sharp beading needle with plenty of thread, and attach firmly to fabric. Pick up as many beads as you need to make the fringe the correct length.

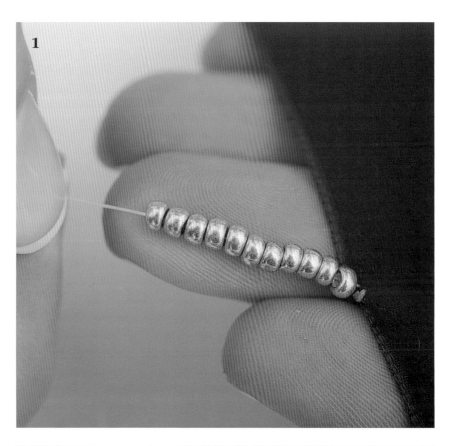

2 Use the bottom bead as a "turning" bead, and pass the needle back up through the fringe. Make a stitch at the top.

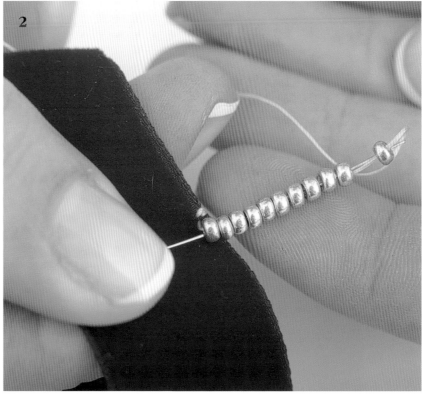

Fringed Bag

I love fringes, they have a life of their own, dancing and shimmying all by themselves. This wonderful fringe is called coral or branching fringe and creates a dense texture very quickly. I was given the lovely coral chips as a gift after a friend went on an expedition to a gem store and remembered my penchant for pink! A ready-made small bag is the basis for this project, so either embellish one you already have or buy a cheap one especially for the project. I made this one from the remnants of a 1920s-style dress made by another friend.

Materials:

Vintage fabric bag approx. 4" by 6"
¼ ounce of coral Delicas
¼ ounce of color-lined coral size 11 seeds
¼ ounce of pearlized coral size 11 seeds
¼ ounce of peach size 10 seeds
2" string of angel coral chips
Fine beading thread

Equipment:

Sharp needle
Scissors

Instructions

1 Thread up a needle with one yard of thread and make a couple of stitches at one bottom corner edge of bag to secure. Thread on about 12 size 10 seeds. Use the bottom bead as a turning bead, and pass the needle up through five beads.

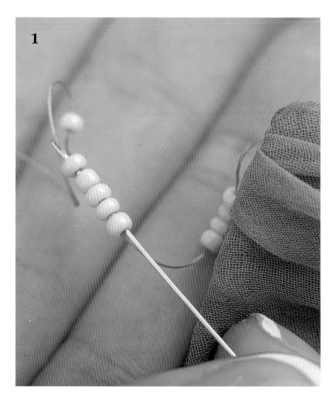

2 Thread on around 12 more seeds. Once more use the bottom bead as a turning bead, and pass the needle up through five beads. Make a final branch in the same way.

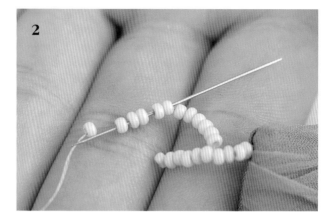

3 On the final branch, pass the needle all the way up to the top of the stem, bypassing the branches, and pull until firm but not too tight or it will not hang correctly. Make a stitch at the top to secure; then move on to another spot ½" away, passing the needle along the inside of the bag.

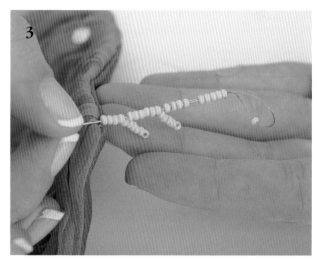

4 Make another stitch to secure, and make a second dangle. Continue all the way along the bottom of the bag, varying the length and quantity of the branches. Finish off the thread at the end. Repeat from step 1 with the pearl coral beads along the bag, too.

5 For the second row of the fringe, continue creating branches in exactly the same way about ½" above the first row, but use the Delicas and the color-lined beads. Be careful not to sew through to the back of the bag. I usually keep my hand inside it to prevent any accidents.

6 To create the coral clumps, thread on about four coral twigs and make a stitch to secure before moving to the next position. Thread on extra beads to the ribbon tie for added decoration if you like.

Cut-Velvet Scarf

This is an amazing fabric base for beading. Although beautiful in its own right, it also lends itself to embroidery as you have a pattern already there that you can enhance, using assorted small beads to greater effect. Cut-velvet is created when different threads are used to weave the pile and the supporting fabric. The pattern is screen printed using a chemical that dissolves the pile threads in the areas it contacts, leaving the background fabric as a contrasting texture, just like magic. This is a freeform project, so add as many or as few beads as you like. I suggest using beads the same color as the pile sections, but you could go for a complete contrast as well.

Materials:

Cut-velvet scarf
½ ounce of matte seed beads size 11
½ ounce of shiny seed beads size 11
½ ounce of Japanese bugle beads
Fine beading thread

Equipment:

Sharp needle
Scissors

Instructions

1 Look at the scarf and decide what motifs will be best enhanced by bead work—choose large distinct areas such as big flowers. I concentrated my embroidery on the bottom half to give weight to the scarf and help it hang nicely. Thread up a needle with 1 yard of fine beading thread and make a couple of little stitches to secure.

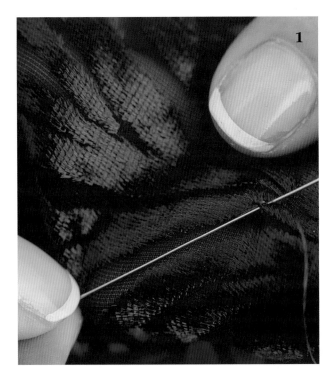

2 To create the angled bugle outlines, which are best used for thick stems and leaves, thread on a bugle, and pass the needle back so that it emerges from the fabric, halfway down the bead.

3 Thread on another bugle, and place it so that it lies parallel to the first. Pass the needle down and up through the fabric again, halfway down the second bugle, and repeat as necessary.

4 To create the seed bursts in the center of the flowers, couch alternate lengths of seven and four seed beads in a star burst pattern following the shape of the petals. See basic techniques for details of couching.

5 To create the beaded buds, thread on three seed beads. Pass the needle down through the fabric to emerge at right angles from the row of beads.

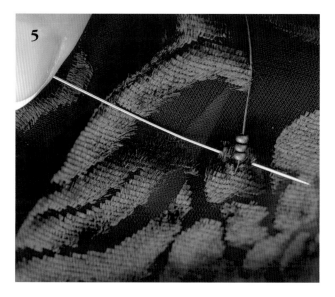

6 Thread a seed; then pass the needle through the center bead of the three. Add on another seed, and maintaining the straight line, pass the needle down through the fabric once more.

7 Continue embellishing quite heavily until you are happy with the result. It is better to embellish fewer motifs in a denser way than to spread your needle work too thinly over a large area. Secure the thread firmly by making a few tiny stitches on top of each other in an inconspicuous place.

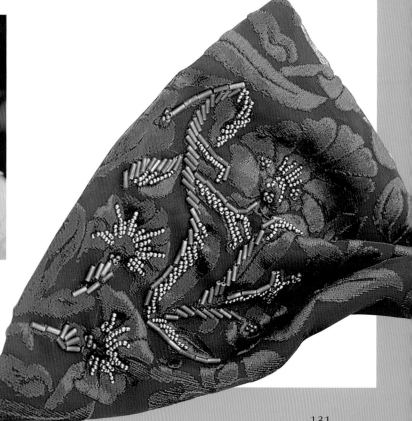

Bead Weaving

*In the same way that knitting and crochet have a repertoire of stitches so does
beading. Unlike traditional weaving no loom is required, just a needle and thread,
that loop and attach one small bead to another in a wide variety of techniques.
New stitches are discovered all the time, as well as old favorites learned from
generations of traditional work passed down through families of beaders.*

As well as creating large areas of flat cloth and braid, bead weaving can be used three dimensionally to make wonderful sculptures. These may be either freestanding, using different sizes of beads or by the careful additions of further same-sized rocailles to shape the pieces. I have seen complete three-dimensional teddy bears, shoes, flowers, and even a Dalek all created by bead weaving. Some sculptures are created by tightly covering an existing object with a flat stitch such as peyote or brick stitch. Stitches can also be used to create shaped necklaces and bracelets, so the possibilities are truly endless.

Different cultures have their own stitches which are often used in traditional dress or objects. Peyote, a tightly woven stitch, is descended from the Native American bead stitch used to cover ceremonial regalia. Ndebele or herringbone comes from South Africa and resembles a herringbone pattern. Netting with beads has been used since Egyptian times when whole netted dresses were created. In Eastern Europe, very elaborate netted necklaces are worn with traditional costumes on national holidays, and in Afghanistan huge tassels are covered with a netted skirt for extra decoration.

Bead weaving is the area in which many bead artists feel they can express themselves. Variations on just about every stitch exist—there is tubular peyote, flat even count peyote, two drop peyote, flat odd count peyote, and so on. Some are easier to master than others; spiral stitch is a particularly rewarding first stitch, whereas odd count peyote is more challenging.

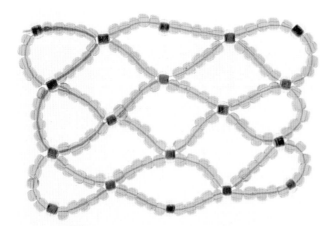

Above: Netted bead weaving
Left: Spiral rope weaving

Each stitch has its own little idiosyncrasies and its own strengths and weaknesses. Peyote stitch, for example, is flexible only in one direction, while brick stitch which looks similar from a distance is totally flexible. The ever useful netting can expand and contract to fit any rounded form.

Seed beads in assorted sizes are the main type used for bead weaving, as they have no sharp edges and a large central hole—useful as the needle and thread has to pass through several times during the weaving process. Delicas are popular for the tighter stitches as they give such a smooth perfect

Below: A brick stitch pendant
Above and Below Right: Spiral rope stitch

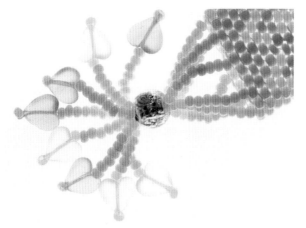

interlocking weave. The needle used is a very long, fine, sharp one. The most common thread is a very fine strong thread stolen from upholstery manufacturers, but any fine strong thread is usable.

Bicone crystals have recently become popular in Japan for lovely woven projects, using transparent nylon wire to create three-dimensional clusters and motifs, from flowered hearts to twinkling stars. Hemp thread projects and macramé are really more knotwork than bead weaving but a lot of similar working practices apply.

Such complicated-looking pieces can seem daunting but they are not as difficult as they seem, I promise! Start slowly and have a go at a few lengths of the basic stitches first. Hold the work in your nondominant hand and the needle and thread in the other. It is important while weaving to make sure the thread is pulled firm after the addition of each bead, as if the tension is loose, it will make the piece almost impossible to continue with. Keep adjusting your hand until you find a comfortable way to work while keeping that firm tension. Eventually it will become second nature.

The complete contingent of bead weaving stitches is so vast that I feel I have only scratched the surface myself; the important thing is to keep trying out new stitches. Square stitch, brick stitch, peyote, spiral rope, ndebele, chevron chain, netting—all have whole books devoted to them, so just have a go. You will soon develop your personal favorites and your own way of doing them. If something is "wrong" but looks good anyway, maybe you have invented a new stitch!

Basic Bead-Weaving Techniques

Stopper bead

1 Thread a small bead using a needle from right to left; then pass the needle back through the bead from right to left again, creating a loop.

2 Repeat once or twice for a firmer stop; be careful not to pass the needle through the thread, just the bead.

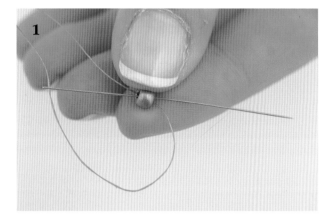

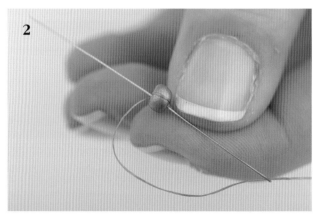

Knots

Square or reef knot (for two ends)

1 Cross the left-hand thread over the right-hand thread, and wrap right around.

2 Now cross the right-hand thread over the left-hand thread, and pull up through the hole. Tighten the knot.

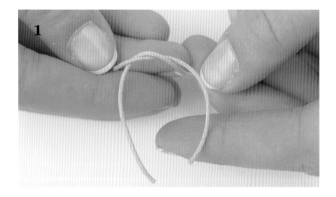

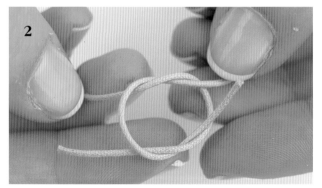

Surgeon's knot (for two ends)

1 Cross the left-hand thread over the right-hand thread, and wrap right around.

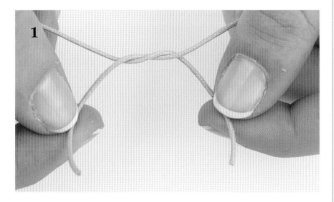

2 Now cross the right-hand thread over the left-hand one, and pull up through the hole.

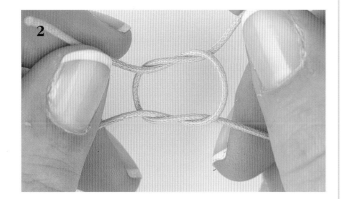

3 Wrap underneath, and pull up through the hole again.

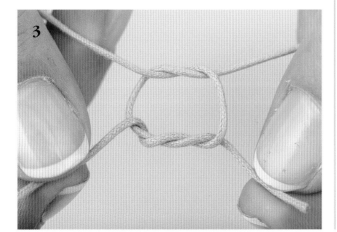

Netting

Different numbers of beads can be used in each netted piece; these are instructions for a three-bead netting pattern.

1 Fasten on a stopper bead; then thread on a bead of the first color (A), three of the second color (B), one A, three Bs, and so on to the length of your piece, ending with an A bead.

2 Thread on one B, one A, and one B, and pass the needle through the A bead of the first row. Repeat this sequence back down the row.

3 At the end add two Bs, one A, and one B, and pass the needle through the A bead of the second row. Continue to the end of the row with one A, one B, and one A. Repeat from step 2 as necessary.

Spiral rope

1 Thread a sharp beading needle with a length of thread. Place a stopper bead on the end of the thread by looping back through the bead. Thread on four size 10 seed beads for the core (A), then three in a contrasting color (B). Thread the needle back up through the four A beads, creating a loop.

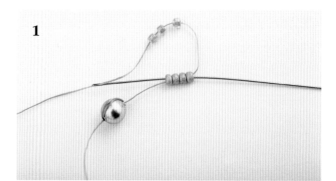

2 Thread on one A bead and three Bs. Pass the needle up through the top four A beads, leaving out the bottom one.

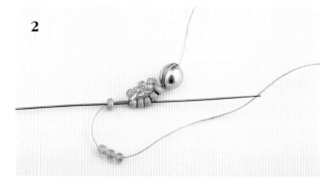

3 Repeat step 2, making sure your outside beads always lie either to the right or the left of the previous row, or it will not build up the spiral properly. Continue until you have a rope the right length.

Peyote stitch

Peyote stitch can be created as even or odd count and can be flat or in a tube. These instructions are for flat even count peyote.

1 Thread a sharp beading needle with a length of fine beading thread. Place a stopper bead on the end of the thread by looping back through the bead. Thread an even number of contrasting beads in the pattern A, B, A, B, A, B, A, B, to the right width of your piece.

2 Add another bead, B, and pass the needle back down through the next to last bead, an A. Add another B bead and missing the next B bead along pass the needle once more through the A bead. Repeat all the way down the row.

3 To make third row, pick up an A bead, and pass needle through B bead. Repeat up row, picking up A beads and going through Bs, keeping tension firm. Continue from step 2 until it is right size.

Attaching a thread

1 When you have about 3" of thread left, cut a new length and tie a square or surgeon's knot close to the beads.

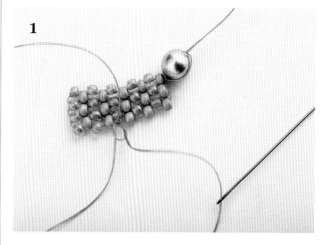

2 Weave the end threads up and down in a zigzag pattern back through the work till secure; then trim.

Finishing the thread

1 Weave the end thread up and down in a zigzag pattern back through the work, and when totally secure, trim close to the beads.

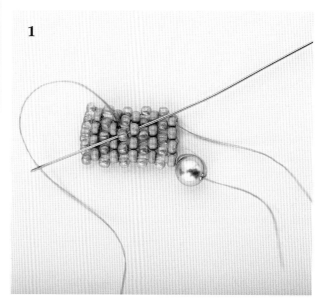

Spiral Rope Bracelet

This bracelet was for my mother-in-law, Jacqui, in her favorite golden colors. She belongs to a bewildering assortment of societies and often goes out to lunch meetings and smart evening dinner parties. I created this for her as an icebreaker, not that she needs one! But you can't really miss such a fabulous bracelet and once spotted it has to be commented on. The spiral rope is so easy to stitch, all the impressive size grading comes from simply using bigger beads in the center section.

Materials:

T-bar clasp
½ ounce of bronze size 9 seed beads
¼ ounce of gold size 10 seed beads
60 small gold beads (size 6)
40 x 4mm transparent gold crystals
10 x 4mm gold pearls
Fine or strong nylon thread

Equipment:

Fine sharp beading needle
Scissors

Instructions

1 Cut and thread up a 1½ yard length of nylon thread. Thread a firm stopper bead as described in basic techniques, leaving a tail of 6". Thread five gold and six bronze seeds. To start the spiral rope, pass the needle up through the five gold seeds.

2 Thread a gold seed and six bronze seeds, and work a spiral rope stitch with one gold and six bronze seeds, as described in basic techniques, for 20 rows, passing the needle always through the top five gold beads.

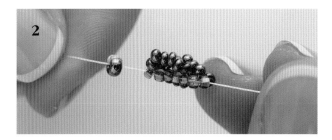

3 For the next section, thread on a gold seed, two bronze seeds, a small gold bead, and two bronze seeds. Pass the needle up through the top five gold seed beads as before. Work spiral stitch with this sequence for 10 rows.

4 The next threading sequence is a gold seed, bronze seed, gold bead, crystal, gold bead, and a bronze seed. Pass the needle up through the top five gold seeds as before. Work spiral stitch with this sequence for 10 rows.

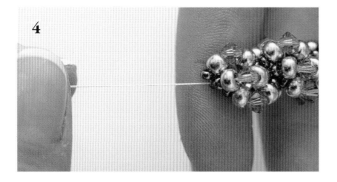

6 Repeat the threading sequence and number of rows from step 4, then step 3, and finally step 2. To add clasp, thread on three bronze seeds, the clasp, and three more seeds. Pass the needle around through the seeds and clasp once more for strength.

5 The center section has no gold bead or bronze seeds—it is simply a gold seed, crystal, 4mm pearl, and crystal. Work spiral stitch with this sequence for ten rows. If you have to add thread, do so using a square knot and weave the ends in, as described in basic techniques.

7 Weave the needle around and around, following in the path of the spiral rope stitches to secure the thread. Trim the thread when you feel it is secure. Unthread the stopper bead and add the clasp using this tail on the other side, securing and trimming as before.

Daisy Chain Anklet

As summer draws near, I look for the little pink edged daisy flowers. I think they are lovely and spent many a happy hour chaining them together as a girl, and was always sad when they wilted. At last I have a solution! This daisy chain will always stay perky. What a great present for a little girl. The pearls are high quality fakes made from crystal; if you use another sort make sure the pearl coating won't chip off.

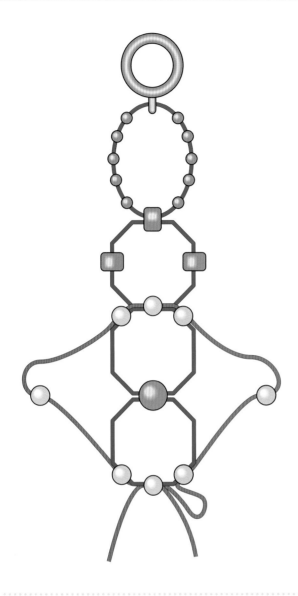

Materials:

Toggle clasp
Eight 6mm lemon pearls
64 x 4mm cream pearls
20 jade tumble chips
¼ ounce of size 10 jade seed beads
40" strong nylon thread

Equipment:

Two sharp needles
Scissors

Instructions

1 Thread each end of the nylon thread with the needles. On the right needle, thread one side of the clasp and five seed beads. On the left needle, thread five seeds beads and a tumble chip.

2 Pass the right-hand needle from right to left through the tumble chip so that the threads cross within it. Thread a tumble chip on each needle.

3 Cross the threads by passing one needle from left to right and the other from right to left through a 4mm pearl.

4 Add a 4mm pearl on each needle, and cross the threads through a 6mm lemon pearl.

5 Next thread on a 4mm pearl on each side, and cross through a 4mm pearl. Pass what is now the right-hand needle, clockwise through the next pearl along, and add a 4mm pearl to fill the gap.

6 Continue passing the needle clockwise around the pearls adding another 4mm in the left-side gap. Cross threads once more through the top pearl.

7 Thread two seeds, a tumble chip, and two seeds, and repeat the flower sequence from step 3. Continue this flower and leaf sequence until you have eight flowers.

8 Finally, thread a tumble chip on each needle, and cross through another chip. On the right-hand needle, pick up five seeds, the other side of the clasp, and five more seeds. Pass the needle through the tumble chip, and go up through all the seeds and clasp to reinforce it.

9 Tie a square knot, and weave the ends of the thread round the flowers in opposite directions. Trim any remaining thread.

Buried Bugle-Bead Necklace

This long 1920s-style necklace is punctuated by clusters of exciting beaded shapes, which look fabulous but are actually terribly easy to make. I have constructed three types using the same technique but with different beads each time, to give you an idea of the possibilities. As for the necklace itself, it could be worn flapper style as a long string or wrap it twice around the neck for a shorter but denser bead necklace. You could even use it as a bracelet or bag strap—talk about versatile!

Materials:

½ ounce of size 10 green seeds
½ ounce of size 10 purple seeds
½ ounce of size 10 blue seeds
½ ounce of 10mm silver bugles
½ ounce of size 7 blue and green seeds
½ ounce of 4mm blue fire-polished
½ ounce of 4mm green fire-polished
½ ounce of 4mm AB crystals
Strong nylon bead thread

Equipment:

Sharp needle
Scissors

Instructions

1 Cut 2 yards of thread. Thread on a stopper bead very securely as described in basic techniques, about 4" from the end.

2 To create the purple cluster, thread on a blue seed, a bugle, and a blue seed.

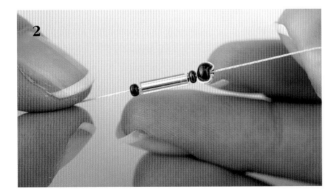

3 Next thread on two purple seeds, a crystal, and two seeds. Pass the needle up through the seed-bugle-seed creating a loop and tighten.

4 Repeat step 3 four more times; then thread on thirty size 10 green seeds.

5 To make the green cluster, thread on a purple seed, a bugle, and a purple seed. Next thread on a green size 7 seed, a purple size 10 seed, a green fire polish, a purple seed, and a green seed. Pass the needle up through the seed-bugle-seed, creating a loop, and tighten. Repeat four more times. Thread on 30 size 10 green seeds.

6 For the blue cluster, thread on a blue size 10 seed, a bugle, and a blue seed. Next, thread on a blue size 10 seed, a blue size 7 seed, a blue fire-polished, a blue size 7 seed, and a blue size 10 seed. Pass the needle up through the seed-bugle-seed creating a loop, and tighten. Repeat four more times. Thread on 30 size 10 green seeds.

8 Tie the two ends together with a square knot as described in basic techniques.

7 Repeat the pattern of purple, green, blue, green, purple, green, blue, green, with thirty seeds in between until the necklace is the right length.

Egyptian-Style Netted Necklace

When I was in Egypt on my honeymoon, I saw the most incredible netted necklaces
in the Cairo museum. They were so intricately constructed, it was hard to believe
they had been made as early as 2000 B.C. I knew I just had to make one.
It took a little while to work out how to stitch the top of the necklace tighter, so
it would curve more than the bottom, but the final design of this spectacular necklace
is actually very straightforward to construct. It is extremely time-consuming
however, so be prepared to bead slowly and carefully, for a couple of hours at a time,
over a week or two. The final result is definitely worth being patient.

Materials:

1 ounce of size 9 blue seed beads (b9)
30 antique gold size 7 seed beads (ag7)
½ ounce of bright gold size 7 seed beads (bg7)
1 ounce of antique gold size 5 seed beads (ag5)
½ ounce of blue bugles (bb)
1 ounce of turquoise bugles (tb)
76 x 4mm lapis lazuli beads (ll4)
75 x 4mm green opal crystals (gc4)
Strong bead thread

Equipment:

Sharp needle
Scissors

Instructions

1 Cut a good 2-yard length of thread. Thread on a firm stopper bead as described in basic techniques, and then thread on a b9, ag7, 2 x b9s, ag7, 2 x b9s, bg7, tb, ag7, ll4, ag7, tb, ag7, 2 x b9s, bg7, 3 x b9, bb, ag7, gc4, ag7, 2 x b9s, ag5, 2 x tb, and bg7.

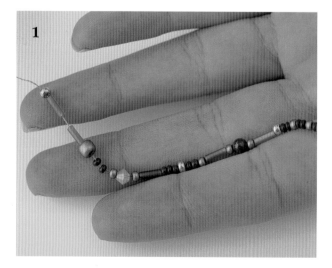

2 Use the bottom bg7 as a turning bead, and thread the needle back up through the 2 x tb, ag5, 2 x b9s, ag7, gc4, and ag7.

148

3 Thread on a bb, 3 x b9s, and pass the needle back up through the bg7 already threaded.

4 Add on 2 x b9s, ag7, tb, ag7, and pass the needle up through the ll4.

5 Thread an ag7, tb, bg7, 2 x b9s, and pass the needle up through the ag7s.

6 Add 2 x b9s, ag7, and pass the needle through the very first bead threaded, the b9.

7 Add 2 x b9s, ag7, and pass the needle down through the top b9 to make a picot edge.

8 Thread 2 x b9s, ag7, and pass the needle down through the top b9.

9 Add on a b9, ag7, 2 x b9s, and pass the needle down through the bg7.

10 Add a tb, ag7, ll4, ag7, tb, and pass the needle down through the ag7.

11 Thread 2 x b9s, bg7, 2 x b9s, and pass the needle down through the third b9.

12 Thread on a bb, ag7, gc4, ag7, b9s, ag5, 2 x tb, and a bg9.

13 Repeat from step 2 until all the lapis and crystal beads have been used. When you have to add thread, tie a square knot and leave the ends long to weave through the pattern, as described in basic techniques. I usually do them all at the end, but you can neaten as you go along if you prefer.

14 Finish your last row with the thread at the top of the necklace. To make the fastenings, thread on 2 x b9 beads, a 4mm lapis bead, and a b9. Using the last bead as a turning bead, turn and thread back through the lapis and two seeds.

15 Weave round the top circle of seeds, and go up and down through the lapis again to reinforce it. Weave the needle down to the next blue seed section, and attach another 4mm lapis in the same way. Finish off the thread by weaving it very securely back through the work.

16 On the other side of the necklace, take off the stopper bead, and thread on around 12 seed beads. Make a loop; attaching it up through the seeds you've already woven. Check the bead fits snugly through the loop—this will be your necklace's fastening so make sure it won't slip out. Adjust the number of seeds as necessary. Go around the loop again for strength and weave down to the next blue seed section, attaching another seed loop in the same way. Finish off the thread by weaving it very securely back through the work.

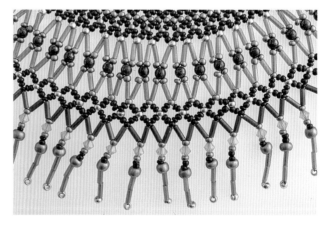

Hemp Choker

*I made this hemp choker for my husband who demanded I design something manly
for him to put his wedding ring on when he goes to the gym. I decided to use all
his favorite earthy colored stones within it, echoing the shapes and colors of the
natural world, as he's a real outdoors type. Hemp is such a fabulous natural fiber,
it's strong and has a great texture but you could also make this necklace from a thin
round leather thong—or for a futuristic look how about a rubber cord? Even a fluffy
textured knitting yarn could look amazing with big crystals instead of beads.*

Materials:

Four 8mm tiger eyes
Four 8mm green aventurines
Four 8mm picture jaspers
Two 8mm goldstone
Two 8mm malachites
One 8mm carnelian
1 yard of strong bead thread
5 yards of hemp yarn
Two leather ends
T-bar clasp
Two 4mm jump rings

Equipment:

Glue
Flat-nosed pliers
Round-nosed pliers
Scissors

Instructions

1 Find the center of the hemp yarn, add the end of the bead thread, and tie an overhand knot to secure all three together. I leave the hemp in a loop so that I can attach the ends to a hook or nail, which makes the knots much easier to tie.

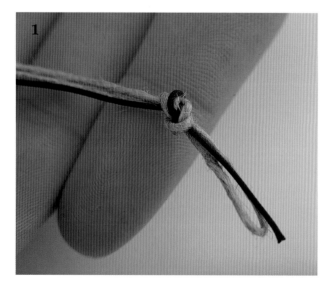

2 Arrange the threads so you have hemp strand each side of the bead cord. Make the left-hand hemp thread into a small loop and cross it above the bead thread. Hold firmly with your thumb and finger where the two threads cross.

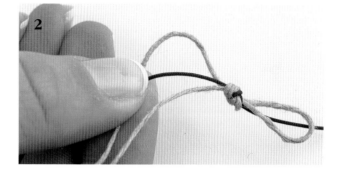

3 Make a loop with the right-hand hemp thread, crossing over the left-hand hemp threads tail, then passing under the central bead thread.

4 Now thread this right-hand hemp up through the loop on the left-hand side. The hemp strands will now have changed sides and the bead thread will be caught through the center of the knot.

5 Gently pull the knot until it is firm but not tight. Practice a bit until you find the correct tension—just like knitting everyone will knot differently.

7 Thread a tiger eye bead onto the central bead thread, and pass the hemp either side to work a knot directly under it, holding the bead in place. Continue knotting another 10 times and add a green aventurine bead. Then continue knotting and threading beads in this sequence: picture jasper, tiger eye, green aventurine, goldstone, malachite, picture jasper, carnelian, picture jasper, malachite, goldstone, green aventurine, tiger eye, picture jasper, green aventurine, and tiger eye.

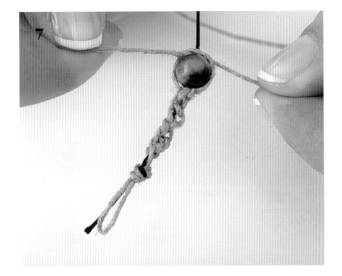

6 Repeat from step 1 until you have 10 knots. It will begin to gently spiral clockwise. Try to keep all the knots the same size and firmness to create a smart uniform piece.

8 Finish with ten knots of spiral and knot threads together. Remove the rope from hook and trim both ends ¼" from the knot. Put a dab of glue on one end, and place in a leather end. Close the leather end around it with flat-nosed pliers. Repeat on other side.

9 Attach the T-bar clasp with a jump ring, twisting to open, as described in basic techniques.

Netted Bead Choker

This bead is an exotic treasure, a delicious Fabergé egg of Russian-style glamour. After trying this design with seeds I ended up with a bead the size of a golf ball, so I strongly advise keeping with the Delicas. They are so tiny they don't overwhelm the bead. As well as a necklace, it could be used as a key fob or tree decoration, or even as the head of a tassel or a light pull. This is a six bead netting design, which creates a very loose and stretchy net; you could also try a tighter weave of three bead netting for a smaller, less ostentatious bead.

Materials:

1" long oval wooden bead
14 x 3mm crystals
¼ ounce of size 10 seed beads
¼ ounce of Delicas
Nylon thread
1½ coils memory wire, necklace size
Two end caps

Equipment:

Glue
Scissors
Sharp needle

Instructions

1 Cut 1½ yards of nylon thread, leaving a 3" tail, and thread on a stopper bead, as described in basic techniques. Thread on: seed bead, five Delicas, seed, five Del., crystal, five Del., crystal, five Del., seed, five Del., seed, five Del., seed, and five Del.

2 Pass the needle up through the second crystal, creating a loop of beads at the end of the string. Pull the thread tight.

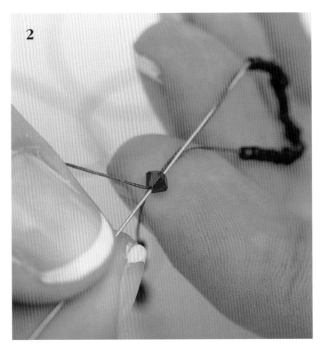

3 Add five Delicas, a crystal, and five Delicas, and pass the needle through the second seed bead that you threaded.

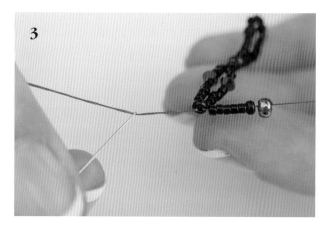

4 Add five Delicas, a seed, five Delicas, a seed, and five Delicas. Pass needle down through top crystal.

5 Add five Delicas, a crystal, and five Delicas, and pass the needle through the bottom-right seed bead.

6 Add five Delicas, seed, five Delicas, seed, and five Delicas, and repeat from step 2.

7 Repeat until you have used all the crystals. When the net is in front of you, with the stopper bead at the top left-hand side, your needle should be emerging from the bottom-right seed bead.

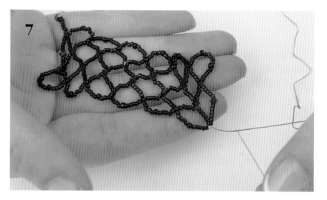

8 To join the net together into a tube, thread five Delicas, seed, and five Delicas, and pass the needle up through the bottom-left seed.

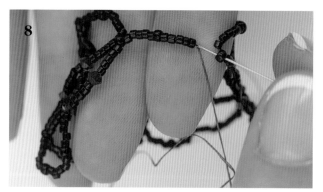

9 Thread five Delicas, and pass the needle through the last crystal threaded.

10 Add five Delicas, and pass the needle through the first crystal threaded. Add five more Delicas, and pass needle through the opposite seed bead. Thread five more Delicas, and pass the needle through the first bead threaded.

11 Add a Delica, and pass the needle through each top seed bead adding a Delica between each. Pull tight and go around the circle again.

12 Weave the thread down the netting, emerging through a seed bead. Repeat step 11, but before you pull tight, insert the bead. Weave all the ends up and down in the work, and trim when secure.

13 To create the choker, glue an end on the memory wire with epoxy glue. Thread seed or Delica beads halfway along; add the big bead; and continue to thread seeds. Finish the wire by gluing another end on.

Garnet Cross

In Tudor times, fabulous jewel encrusted crosses were owned by the wealthy English noblemen of the day, proclaiming both their devotion to God and their household riches. As explorers brought back new and exciting gems from their discovered lands, ever more splendid jewelry was designed and presented to royalty. I designed a slightly less ostentatious piece which nevertheless retains a flavor of the courts of Henry VIII and Elizabeth I. The garnet and crystal cross is woven in the Japanese style that, although it looks fabulously intricate, is in fact very simple to create. It uses just one very clever technique: crossing two threads in opposite directions through a bead. Many gorgeous Japanese crystal pendant motifs are created in this way, just using seeds and crystals to produce a huge variety of shapes from hearts to horseshoes.

Materials:

20 x 4mm garnet beads
48 x 4mm crystals
¼ ounce of size 10 seed beads
Nylon beading wire, approx. 1 yard
Strong beading thread
36" strand of tumble chip garnets

Equipment:

Scissors
Glue

Instructions

1 Thread on three crystals, and move them down to the center of the nylon beading wire. You will be working with both ends of the wire at the same time. Take the right-hand thread, and pass it from right to left through a fourth crystal. Take the left-hand thread, and pass it from left to right through the fourth crystal, too, so that the threads cross inside it. Pull the threads tight, creating a circle.

2 Thread a crystal on each wire, and cross the threads through a seventh crystal. Next thread a crystal on each, and cross wires through a garnet bead. Continue this pattern until you have four garnet beads in sequence.

3 On the right-hand thread, pick up a garnet, a crystal, a garnet, and three crystals. Pass the thread back through the second garnet, making the three crystals into a loop.

4 Add on a crystal, and pass the thread through the first crystal to make a second loop. Repeat from step 3 with the left-hand wire to make the second arm of the cross.

5 Pass the two threads left and right through a garnet bead, and add a crystal on each thread.

6 Continue the weaving pattern as illustrated, ending with a crystal on each thread.

7 Cross the wires through the crystal at the end so that the cross is now joined at the top and bottom.

8 Continue one thread through the next two of these bottom crystals. The threads should now be emerging from equal crystals on opposite sides of the front and back of the cross.

9 To weave the front and back together, thread each end up through the next woven crystal, and cross them through a seed bead. Thread each up through the next crystal, and then cross through another seed bead.

10 Continue all the way around the edge of the cross. At the top, pass both threads through one crystal, and continue as before. At the bottom, tie a square knot, and dab on epoxy glue.

11 Thread half the garnets onto the strong bead thread and string on the cross through the top crystal. Continue threading all the rest of the garnets, and tie the strands with a square knot. Pass the thread ends back down through the tumble chips to neaten.

Frilled Peyote Bracelet

Who needs diamonds? While I occasionally think it might be nice to own a big diamond bracelet, I have to admit this seeded cuff sparkles like a starlet on Oscar night. Its secret is in the silver-lined seed beads, which when woven in this three-dimensional form seem to sparkle even more than usual. Not being able to help myself, I added a glitzy clasp and yet more crystals—suddenly what might otherwise be a clever but dull bracelet turned into an expensive looking work of art, which friends keep asking to borrow.

Materials:

½ ounce of size 10 silver-lined seed beads
Six sew-on crystals
Crystal set clasp, two hole
Four ½" pieces of gimp/French wire
Strong nylon thread
Thread conditioner

Equipment:

Sharp needle
Scissors

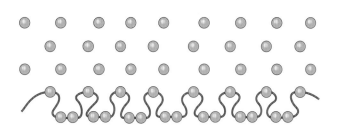

Instructions

1 Cut 40" of nylon thread, and thread on a stopper bead as described in basic techniques, about 15" from the end. Thread up the needle with the other end, and pick up 80 seed beads.

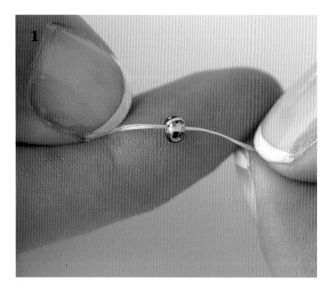

2 Pick up another seed bead, and create peyote stitch down the length of the row, as described in basic techniques. Work two more rows of peyote up and down. If you run out of thread, add some more as described in basic techniques.

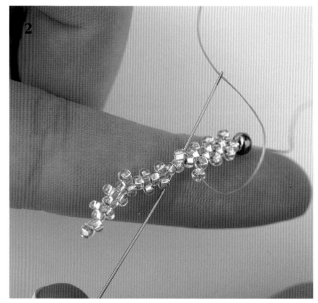

3 Continue with another row of the stitch, but pick up and add two beads in each gap instead of just one. This will create the frill on one side, so keep the tension tight but expect it to twirl all over the place.

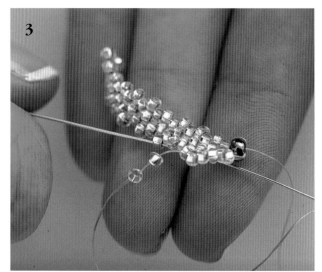

4 Thread the nylon thread up and down along the top edge of the weave, and work a row of peyote along the non-frilled edge. Then make the frill on this side in the same way as described in step 3. Finish with the thread emerging from one corner.

5 Thread a piece of gimp and pass it through one end of the clasp. Thread back through a seed bead and work the needle up and down, zigzagging through the seeds until it is totally secure. Repeat for the other corner of the weave and the other hole of the clasp.

6 Weave the needle down the seeds, and sew on a crystal in the center of the strip, sewing straight through the seeds. When it's totally secure, weave down ½" passing the needle through the beads and sew on another crystal—repeat for a third sparkle.

7 Finally attach the other end of the clasp and crystals in exactly the same way, and remember to buy yourself a new evening dress!

Art Deco Bracelet

*Stone donuts are traditional shapes for pendants in China and while I love them,
I can't often think of enough interesting things to do with them. Then one day, I was
looking at Art Deco shapes of jewelry and was suddenly inspired to create a peyote stitch
setting for this lovely pink stone ring. The odd count peyote stitch is slightly more
complicated than the even count version described in basic techniques. It takes
a bit of practice, but it's worth persevering because it's so useful. It's also essential if you
have want a strip with a symmetrical pattern, as we do for this project.*

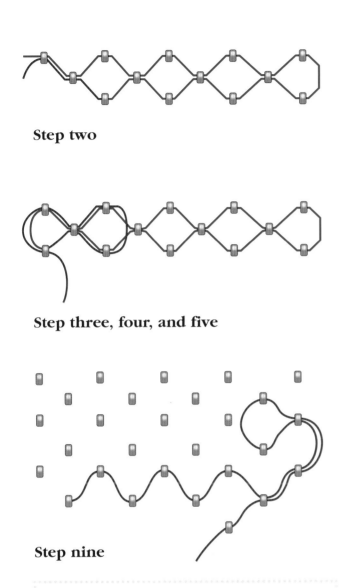

Step two

Step three, four, and five

Step nine

Materials:

Stone donut 1¼" across with ½" hole
Lobster clasp
Strong nylon thread
Two 4mm rondelles
Four 4mm pink pearls
Four 4mm crystals
¼ ounce of main color Delicas
¼ ounce of five other colors of Delicas

Equipment:

Long beading needle

Instructions

1 Using a 3-foot length of strong nylon thread, place a stopper bead on the thread about 1½ foot from the end. You will return to this piece of thread to add the clasp. To begin the peyote stitch, thread on nine Delicas.

2 Add a tenth Delica and weave the needle from right to left, through the eighth bead. Add a Delica, and pass needle through the sixth Delica. Add one more, and pass the needle through the fourth Delica. Add another, and pass the needle through the second and the first beads.

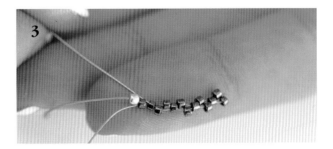

3 Thread on a Delica (number 14), and pass the needle up from left to right through the second and third Delicas of the original row.

4 Pass the needle back down through numbers 13, two, and one.

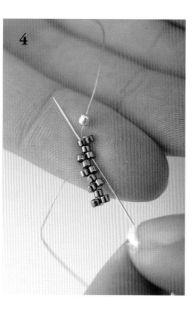

5 Pass the needle from left to right through the last added bead (number 14). You will now have a ladder and are ready to start the third row.

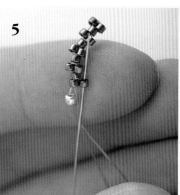

6 For the third row, weave a Delica from left to right, through each sticking out bead of the previous row.

7 Weave down from right to left to the last space (bead number 22). Pass the needle through the last two beads (numbers 15 and 14); add a bead; and pass the needle left to right through 14 and 13. Pass the needle down from right to left through 17, 16, and 14, then back from left to right through 15.

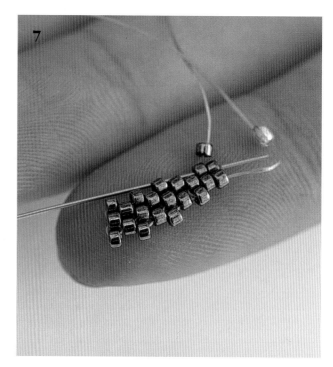

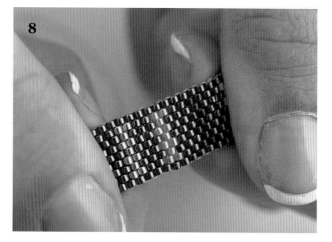

8 Repeat the bead-adding sequence from step 6, using the different colored Delicas, until you are ready start the decrease.

9 To decrease, finish the row so that you have four beads sticking out and the needle emerging from the end bead. Pass the needle from right to left through the last two beads of the previous row, and thread needle back from left to right up through the last bead added.

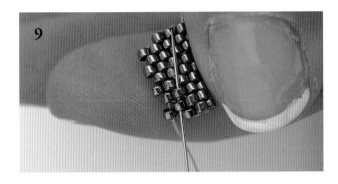

10 Continue weaving the thinner row in the same way to the end of the chart. When you finish the last row, be sure to leave the thread end nice and long.

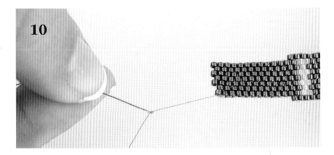

11 Wrap the thin end around the donut, and attach it like a zipper by weaving the beads together with the long thread end. Secure thread by weaving back zigzag through the work and trim.

12 On the other end of the strap, unthread the stopper bead and thread on five Delicas, a crystal, Delica, pearl, rondelle, pearl, Delica, crystal, and clasp or jump ring, and then go back down through all the beads to the second crystal.

13 Add five Delicas, and weave your thread down through the bottom Delica, around and around through the work until you are in a position to repeat step 12, reinforcing the clasp. Weave the thread end securely through the work, and trim. Make and attach the other strap in the same fashion, and add other side of the clasp in same way, too.

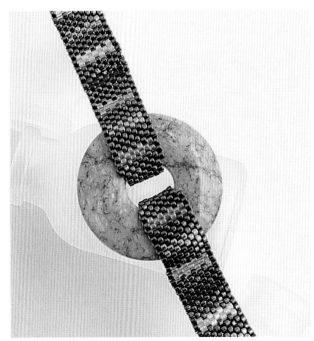

Designing Your Own Jewelry

All designers have their own preferred ways of working—some meticulously draw out a clear plan of their end product, including every component and how it will be joined together, others start with a pile of beads and a picture in their head and see where it goes! No matter how they work, every designer I've met is a secret horder, building up a collection of useful and beautiful beads to draw from, often buying unusual pieces when they see them and deciding exactly how to use them at a later date.

This is not to say that designers randomly buy every bead they see. They will often have a collection of pieces forming in their mind when they go bead shopping, or even a specific type of beaded work that is instantly recognizable as their style. We are often drawn back time and time again to specific colors or shapes, so try to analyze why you like the things you do. Is it because they are dainty, chunky, or spiky? Are you always drawn to flowers or do you always buy blue? Two people given exactly the same set of beads will think of very different ways to use them, reflecting their own tastes and style.

A designer's aim is to cultivate something in their work that makes it instantly recognizable as theirs. While they will often be inspired by other people's ideas, they will take the ball and run with it, often ending up with a product far removed from their original inspiration. It is a good idea to start keeping a scrapbook of images you like, such as pieces of jewelry seen in fashion magazines, colors that look good together; even the shapes of objects completely unrelated to jewelry may spark off a new idea.

I like to carry a small notebook around with me wherever I go, just to doodle in with a cheap pen. Don't worry about the artistic style, no one will ever see your ideas book, and you can always jot down notes in words, as well as pictures, if you don't feel confident with drawing. A good starting point for inspiration is often the past. I like to look at historical pieces in museums and auction catalogs, particularly 1920s and Victorian fashion papers. But you might feel enthused by chunky jade of the Incas or the subtle floral designs of ancient Japan. The Internet is a wonderful resource for designers, just put in a few key words and have a wander. Remember a piece that was originally made by silversmithing can often be reinterpreted in beads.

Another good design tool available from art shops is a color wheel; this shows colors with their complementary and harmonious hues. A complementary color is one which we often think of as opposite, orange and blue, purple and yellow, red and green. A harmonious color is one similar to the main color, blue and purple, yellow and orange for example. Of course not every shade of blue looks good with every shade of orange—try putting different beads next to each other and group tubes of seed beads in sets that look nice to you. Look for the complementary colors that will provide a zingy contrast as well as those that blend in harmony.

You might like the simplicity of classical Greek patterns or fall for the looping swirls of the Art Nouveau. Keep drawing shapes and thinking about what methods you could use to bring these ideas to life. A simple Greek key pattern could be created for a bracelet on a loom but how will you do it up? You could use a bead and loop, or a smart clasp, or attach it to ribbon and sew hook-and-eye fastening tape to create a seamless band. There are many possibilities and all give a different feel to the work.

Don't attempt too much to begin with—if you start a long and complicated project without a clear idea of how you are going about it or how long it is likely to take, you're likely to get discouraged halfway through and never finish it. Create a few smaller designs to try out your ideas and techniques first. Don't be afraid to go wrong—if it doesn't work, put that idea aside and start again. Good design is all about trial and error!

Left: Necklace by Pauline Holt
Below: Beaded charm bracelet

Gallery of Artists

There are millions of us beaders out there—some bead full-time while others use their beads as a creative outlet as and when they feel inspired. Beads have inspired many creative geniuses through history, both in jewelry design and as clothing embellishment. These are a just a few contemporary bead artists who all push forward the boundaries for bead design.

A design by Jeannette Slack

LYNNE HARDY first discovered the joys of beading at an amulet purse workshop at her local embroiderers' guild. She is particularly interested in Art Deco jewelry, and many of her pieces use that as inspiration, joining exciting geometric shapes with bold and unusual color combinations. She is currently retraining as a teacher so that she can share her knowledge of beads and embroidery with us all. These stunning designs use beadweaving stitches of brick, netting, and square stitch, along with peyote and fringing.

➤ She can be contacted on beadily@rkh1.demon.co.uk

JEANETTE SLACK'S love affair with beaded jewelry began many years ago when she came across a beading supplies catalog. While marveling at the exquisite and brightly colored beads, she decided right there and then she wanted to purchase everything in the book! She is now a self-confessed bead addict, finding inspiration from the beads themselves, which she collects from all over the globe. The beaded jewelry displayed here is created using tiger tail secured with crimps, and it incorporates intricately beaded shapes, as well as smart wire work techniques.

➤ See her designs at www.piglut.co.uk

DENISE PIGGIN is a costume maker specializing in historical reproductions of Victorian garments. She takes her inspiration from the colors and textures of the fabrics she uses in her dressmaking, choosing beading styles, colors, and arrangements to complement and set off each project, creating exciting highlights that draw the eye. She uses a variety of bead-work designs and techniques to accent and finish costumes or to create striking focal points for entire outfits. Beaded back stitch is used on the impressive bead-work cross, and the bead work on the hats is a combination of Japanese crystal weaving and fringing.

➤ Email her at denise@pootleproductions.com

Lynne Hardy (above) and Denise Piggin (below)

A Jema Hewitt design (left)

together with Japanese-style crystal weaving for unusual and original jewelry.

➠ Her web site is www.bridal-originals.co.uk

PAULINE HOLT of Jazzy Lily Hot Glass Jewelry has always been excited about color, especially colored glass. Even before her first glass-making course in 1998, she knew she had found her ultimate passion. The challenge of heating glass and carefully shaping it into miniature works of art that can be worn is still magical to her. She now regularly teaches glass bead making for beginners, sharing the thrill when they create their first bead. Her gorgeous glass creations are set off by Bali silver beads, crystals, and an elegant macramé knotted cord made from fine rayon thread.

➠ See her beads at www.jazzylily.com

ISOBELLE BUNTING has been beading for six years since retiring from teaching. She is a founding member of a bead workers guild and for the last two years has been its chairman. She enjoys beading three-dimensional objects best, often using nature as a source for her designs (particularly flowers, plants, and water), and she uses a wide variety and colors of beads to re-create objects. She finds the challenge of overcoming the constraints that beading present very exciting. The piece on the right was made using separate netted sections in seed beads and crystals, which were strung together.

➠ You can contact her at econfsb@aol.com

JEMA HEWITT creates sparkling designs from crystals and semiprecious stones. Her work reflects her theatrical background and is influenced by vintage designs and haute couture dresses—her tiaras especially are highly sought after by brides. As well as writing articles and books, she exhibits in several galleries and runs workshops on everything from corsetry to crystal bracelets. The tiaras use wire twisted with precious beads, while the chokers are created using fringing and embroidery techniques,

Jema Hewitt

Pauline Holt

Isobelle Bunting

A Jema Hewitt tiara

Resource Guide

The following list of manufacturers and associations is meant to be a general guide to additional industry and product-related sources. It is not intended as a listing of products and manufacturers represented by the photographs in this book.

UNITED STATES

Ackfeld Mfg.
P.O. Box 1268
Liberty, MO 64069
(888) 272-3135
www.ackfeldwire.com

Aldastar Corp.
70 Spruce St.
Paterson, NJ 07501
(973) 742-6787
www.aldastar.com

Artisan's Choice
2066 Wineridge Pl.
San Diego, CA 92029
(760) 480-0175
www.artisanschoice.com

Beadalon
205 Carter Dr.
West Chester, PA 19382
(610) 692-7551
www.beadalon.com

Beader's Paradise
4201 Guinn Rd.
Knoxville, TN 37031
(865) 927-3800

The Beadery
105 Canonchet Rd.
Hope Valley, RI 02832
(401) 539-2438
www.thebeadery.com

Beads World Inc.
1384 Broadway
New York, NY 10018
www.beadsworldusa.com

The Beadworks Group
www.beadworks.com

Black Hills Software
(Bead Wizard beading
design software)
www.beadwizard.com

Cheep Trims
5524 Alcoa Ave.
Vernon, CA 90058
(877) BUY-TRIM
www.cheaptrims.com

Cottage Rose Collections
(watch faces)
P.O. Box 32524
Tucson, AZ 85751
www.cottagerosecollec
tions.com

Cousin Corp. of America
12333 Enterprise Blvd.
Largo, FL 33776
(727) 536-3568
www.cousin.com

The Craft Pedlars
1035 S. Shary Circle
Concord, CA 94518
(925) 837-1219
www.pedlars.com

Crafter's Pick
520 Cleveland Ave.
Albany, CA 94710
(510) 526-7616
www.crafterspick.com

Halcraft USA
30 W. 24th St., 9th floor
New York, NY 10010
(212) 376-1580
www.halcraft.com

Flights of Fancy
4005 Mesa Ridge Dr.
Fort Worth, TX 76137
(800) 530-8745
www.flightsoffancybou
tique.com

Firefly Beadcrafts
12289 Windcliff Dr.
Davisburg, MI 48350
(248) 634-3649
www.fireflybead.com

GHI Inc.
305 Wildberry Ct., Ste. B-1
Schaumberg, IL 60193
(847) 891-5609
www.beadbuddy.net

Gold Crest
650 Ward Dr.
Santa Barbara, CA 93111
(800) 922-3233
www.goldcrestinc.com

Gutermann of America
8227 Arrowridge Blvd.
Charlotte, NC 28273
(704) 525-7068
www.gutermann.com

Hirschberg Schutz
650 Liberty Ave.
Union, NJ 07083
(908) 810-1111

Jesse James Button and Trim
615 N. New St.
Allentown, PA 18102
(610) 435-8254

Jewelcraft LLC
505 Windsor Dr.
Secaucus, NJ 07094
(201) 223-0804
www.jewelcraft.biz

Roylco, Inc.
3251 Abbeville Hwy.
Anderson, SC 29624
(800) 362-8656
www.roylco.com

Schylling
P.O. Box 513
Rowley, MA 01969
(978) 948-3601
www.schylling.com

CANADA

John Bead Corp.
19 Bertrand Ave.
Toronto, ON M1L-2P3
(416) 757-3287
www.johnbead.com

Magenta
2275 Bombardier
Sainte-Julie, QB J3E-2J9
(450) 922-5253
www.magentastyle.com

Reiner Craft Corp.
765 Beaubien St. E, #108
Montreal, QB H25-1S8
(514) 324-8645
www.reinercraft.com

INTERNATIONAL

Bead Shop
www.beadworks.co.uk

The Bead Shop
4114 N. Oakland Ave.
Milwaukee, WI 53211
(414) 961-9200
www.mailorder-beads.co.uk

The Bead Merchant
www.beadmerchant.co.uk

Celia's Vintage Clothing
www.celias-nottm.co.uk

ASSOCIATIONS
UNITED STATES

American Craft Council
21 S. Eltings Corner Rd.
Highland, NY 12528
(800) 836-3470
www.craftcouncil.org

Arts and Crafts Association
of America
4888 Cannon Woods Ct.
Belmont, MI 49306
(616) 874-1721
www.artsandcraftsassoc.com

Association of Crafts &
Creative Industries
1100-H Brandywine Blvd.
P.O. Box 3388
Zanesville, OH 43702
(740) 452-4541
www.accicrafts.org

Hobby Industry Association
319 E. 54th St.
Elmwood Park, NJ 07407
(201) 794-1133
www.hobby.org

National Craft Association
1945 E. Ridge Rd., Suite
5178
Rochester, NY 14622
(800) 715-9594

CANADA

Canada Craft and Hobby
Association
#24 1410-40 Ave., N.E.
Calgary, AL T2E 6L1
(403) 291-0559

Canadian Crafts Federatopm
c/o Ontario Crafts Council
Designers Walk
170 Bedford Rd., Suite 300
Toronto, ON M5R 2K9
(416) 408-2294
www.Canadiancraftsfederation.ca

Acknowledgments

There are lots of wonderful people who inspired, encouraged, and assisted me through this book, I really couldn't do it without you, so my heartfelt thanks to:

Ma for writing me books when I was little, you always inspire me.

Dad who keeps exciting findings to make fishing flies with and taught me a reef knot.

Sister Roz always the prettiest and most enthusiastic recipient of my trial pieces.

Husband Nik who actually encourages me to buy more beads!

Simon Clay for the gorgeous photographs.

Josephine Lanning, a wonderful and patient hand model.

Rebekah Roberts, my sorcerer's apprentice who beaded as if her life depended on it.

Liz Johnson, my fabulous personal bead shopper.

All at The Bead Shop for beading madness and fun.

Celia, Denise, Isabelle, Jets, Lynne, and Pauline for loaning me their marvelous bead work, you're all so talented.

Frank Hopkinson and all at Chrysalis Books for their support.

Index